YOUR NEXT
MIRACLE

YOUR NEXT MIRACLE

Experiencing the Power of Christ
in Everyday Life

WARREN W. WIERSBE

Baker Books
A Division of Baker Book House Co
Grand Rapids, Michigan 49516

Published by Baker Books
a division of Baker Book House Company
P.O. Box 6287, Grand Rapids, MI 49516-6287

Printed in the United States of America

ISBN 0-8010-6352-3

Library of Congress Cataloging-in-Publication data is on file at the Library of Congress, Washington, D.C.

For current information about all releases from Baker Book House, visit our web site:
http://www.bakerbooks.com

CONTENTS

GOD'S SECOND
GREATEST MIRACLE

*T*he greatest miracle God performs is the salvation of the lost sinner.

Why? Well, for one thing, the miracle of salvation meets the greatest need, for without it sinners are condemned forever. The miracle of salvation also costs the greatest price—the death of Jesus Christ, God's Son, on the cross. God accomplished other miracles simply by an act of His will; He spoke the word, and it was done. But to accomplish the miracle of salvation, God needed a costly sacrifice and gave His own beloved Son to die for the sins of the world.

The miracle of salvation produces the greatest results. Jesus healed the sick and raised the dead, but ultimately they sickened again and died. He fed the hungry, but eventually they hungered again. But when He forgives a repentant sinner, He does a work that lasts for time and eternity.

When sinners turn by faith to Christ, they experience a miracle that makes them the children of God forever.

But God's greatest miracle leads to God's second greatest miracle, *the transforming of His children into the persons He wants them to be*. The new birth isn't the end; it's the beginning. The crisis of the new birth leads to the process of the new life so that believers are more and more "conformed to the image of His Son" (Rom. 8:29 NASB). We discover the gifts and abilities the Lord has given us, and we learn to draw upon the power He provides. We discover how to use those gifts for the good of others and the glory of God. We find ourselves able to do things we never dreamed were possible, and all the while we grow closer to the Lord and experience His love, His forgiveness, and His joy.

All of this happened to the apostle Peter. I've heard people criticize Peter, but they were wrong in doing so. Peter wasn't faultless, but neither are we. Peter was a great man, and Jesus Christ made his life a miracle. Like all of us, he sometimes spoke when he should have listened and acted when he should have waited. But Jesus loved Peter and transformed him from an ordinary fisherman into an extraordinary servant of the Lord. Our Lord's first miracle was turning water into wine, but that was nothing compared with turning Simon "the hearer" into Peter "the rock."

At their first meeting Jesus said to him, "You are Simon son of John. You will be called Cephas" (John 1:42). When you translate Cephas, you get "Peter—a rock." That's God's greatest miracle—turning a piece of common clay into a solid rock! He made Peter's life a miracle, and He can do the same for you.

If you have put your faith in Jesus Christ, you've experienced God's greatest miracle: the new birth. Now it's time to put your life into His hands and experience God's second greatest miracle: letting Him make you into the person He wants you to be. Jesus can heal bodies and stop storms just by saying the word, for everything in creation obeys Him. But to make your life a miracle, He needs your cooperation.

Don't settle for the ordinary Christian life. Let Jesus make your life a miracle.

Without Jesus, Peter might have been a good fisherman, perhaps even a very good one. But he would never have gotten anywhere, would never have learned what a coward he really was, what a confused, then confessing, courageous person he was, even a good preacher (Acts 2) when he needed to be. Peter stands out as a true individual, or better, a true character, not because he had become "free" or "his own person," but because he had become attached to the Messiah and messianic community, which enabled him to lay hold of his life, to make so much more of his life than if he had been left to his own devices.

Stanley Hauerwas and William H. Willimon[1]

When Simon Peter first steps upon the scene he is a rash, impulsive, and impetuous man. One recognizes the slumbering greatness of him; but one feels the boundless possibilities of evil. But Jesus handles him and plays upon him as a master musician might play on his loved instrument, till the chords are wakened into such glorious music that the centuries are ringing with it still.

George H. Morrison[2]

Many, I fear, never see God work for them because they always have a way out—some friend, perhaps, who might help a little if God does not! Most to be pitied are those who, brought to a supreme crisis, still find an avenue of escape. For necessity is the foundation for miracles. To escape the one is to miss the other. Great difficulties are meant only to force us out of ourselves into reliance on Him.

Watchman Nee[3]

one

THE BEGINNING OF MIRACLES

John 1:40-42

Andrew, Simon Peter's brother, was one of the two who heard what John had said and who had followed Jesus. The first thing Andrew did was to find his brother Simon and tell him, "We have found the Messiah" (that is, the Christ). And he brought him to Jesus.

Jesus looked at him and said, "You are Simon son of John. You will be called Cephas" (which, when translated, is Peter).

*T*o appreciate what Jesus did for Simon Peter—and what He can do for you and me—we should first learn what kind of a man Simon was before he met Jesus. His résumé is brief.

- He was born in Bethsaida ("house of fishing") in Galilee (John 1:44).
- He was named after Jacob and Leah's second son, Simeon (in the Greek Simon).
- He was married and lived in Capernaum, where he ran a fishing business with his brother Andrew and his partners James and John (Luke 5:9–10).
- His mother-in-law lived with him and his wife, and so did his brother Andrew (Mark 1:29–31).
- Peter and his wife kept a kosher home (Acts 10:14), but he confessed that keeping the Jewish law was like wearing a yoke (Acts 15:10).

The fact that Simon was a Jew meant that he believed in the true and living God and accepted the Holy Scriptures as God's authoritative Word. He was a son of the covenant and believed in the promise of the Messiah. That he was a fisherman suggests he wasn't afraid of hard work and didn't quit when the going was tough. It's probable that at least seven of our Lord's disciples were fishermen (see John 21:1–3), which meant that He chose men who knew how to work, how to work together, and how to get the job done. Keep in mind that fishing was their vocation and not a pastime. If they didn't catch fish, they didn't pay their bills.

What does Simon Peter's résumé read like today? Encyclopedias devote pages to him, and scholars around the world study his life and epistles and write learned books about him. Every day Christians read about him in the New Testament and get encouragement from the record of his life and ministry. If John is the apostle of love and

Paul the apostle of faith, then Peter is the apostle of hope. In fact, Simon Peter is the very embodiment of hope. Before he met Jesus, Peter was just another Jewish fisherman; but then he met Jesus and everything changed. Peter started living in the future tense, and Jesus made his life a miracle.

A New Beginning

When John the Baptist suddenly appeared at the Jordan River and announced that the kingdom of God was at hand, great numbers of people hastened to hear him. From the king on the throne to the lowliest slave, the nation was shaken by this man and his message. Was it possible that God was speaking to His people again after being silent for four centuries? The Jews had heard the prophet Malachi read in the synagogue, and they were now hoping that his prophecy was being fulfilled. "See, I will send you the prophet Elijah before that great and dreadful day of the Lord comes. He will turn the hearts of the fathers to their children, and the hearts of the children to their fathers" (Mal. 4:5–6). People all over the land temporarily forgot the hopelessness of living under the iron fist of Rome and became excited about the future of their nation. Was John really the promised messenger? Did this mean that the Messiah was soon to come? Will Israel at last inherit the promised kingdom?

The news about John the Baptist traveled rapidly through the land and arrived in Capernaum. Simon Peter and his partners decided to travel to Judea to hear this unusual preacher, who called the Pharisees and Sadducees "a generation of vipers" (Matt. 3:7 KJV) and required repentant sinners to be baptized. The Jews were accustomed to seeing Gentile proselytes baptized when they entered the Jewish faith, but why would God's chosen people, the citizens of the covenant nation, need to be baptized? Not content with hearing secondhand reports, the four men left their boats and nets with their helpers and followed the crowds to the Jordan River.

They wouldn't realize until much later that they were listening to the greatest prophet God ever sent. "A prophet?" asked Jesus. "Yes, I tell you, and more than a prophet. . . . I tell you the truth: Among those born of women there has not risen anyone greater than John the Baptist" (Matt. 11:9, 11). It appears that Peter, Andrew, James, and John were baptized by John the Baptist (Acts 1:21–22) and became his disciples.

But it was not John the Baptist's purpose to gather disciples around himself. His calling was to introduce people to Jesus Christ. "Look, the Lamb of God, who takes away the sin of the world!" (John 1:29). Peter and his friends were devout Jews who knew about Passover lambs and daily sacrifices, but John's declaration introduced something new. John pointed to a Lamb who was sent by God, not chosen by a priest; a Lamb whose blood could take away sin, not just cover it; a Lamb given for the whole world, not just for families in the Jewish nation.

The next day, Andrew and John were standing with John the Baptist, and Jesus passed by. "Look, the Lamb of God!" said the prophet, and Andrew and John followed Jesus and spent the rest of the day with Him. That one interview convinced them that Jesus of Nazareth was indeed their Messiah, and they trusted Him and received new life.

A New Name

Where was Simon Peter when Andrew and John met with Jesus? We don't know, and it's useless to speculate. But his brother Andrew knew where to find him, and find him he did—it was the first thing Andrew did after he left

Jesus. "The first thing Andrew did was to find his brother Simon. . . . And he [Andrew] brought him [Simon] to Jesus" (John 1:41–42). People come to Christ in different ways, but the important thing is that they come to Him. Andrew and John heard the preaching of John the Baptist and followed Jesus, while Simon Peter was brought to Christ by the personal witness of his own brother. It has often been pointed out that wherever you find Andrew in the Gospel of John, he's bringing someone to Jesus: first, his own brother Simon (John 1:41–42), then the little boy with the lunch (6:8–9), and finally the Gentiles who wanted to see Jesus (12:20–22). There are no sermons from Andrew recorded in Scripture, but his example of personal witness has inspired and motivated Christians for centuries.

Was it easy to bring Simon to Jesus? We don't know. He had just become a disciple of John the Baptist and perhaps didn't want to change allegiance. Surely Andrew explained to Simon that the purpose of John the Baptist's ministry was to get people to follow Jesus. John was only a voice (John 1:23), but Jesus was the Word (1:1, 14). John was but a lamp (5:33–35), but Jesus is the Light of the world (1:4–9; 8:12). John's theology was summarized in two statements: "Look, the Lamb of God" (1:36), and "He must become greater; I must become less" (3:30).

When Andrew introduced Simon to Jesus, "Jesus looked at him" (John 1:42). The phrase means that Jesus fixed His eyes on Simon with a penetrating gaze, looking not just at the face of the fisherman but into his heart and his future. (This same word is used when Jesus looked at Simon Peter after the disciple had denied Him; see Luke 22:61.) Jesus wasn't trying to discover whether Simon was worthy to be His disciple, because nobody is worthy. Our relationship with Jesus Christ is wholly of grace. We can't earn salvation, and we certainly don't deserve it. With that look, Jesus immediately understood Simon's strengths and weaknesses—we all have them—

as well as his gifts and potential for leadership. Jesus knew what Simon could do for the work and what the work could do for Simon.

"You are Simon son of John," said Jesus. "You will be called Cephas" (John 1:42). Cephas is Aramaic for "rock"; the Greek form is Peter. The fisherman now had four names: Simeon, Simon, Cephas, and Peter. But the new name signaled a new beginning in his life, just as when God changed Abram to Abraham, Sarai to Sarah, and Jacob to Israel (Gen. 17:5, 15; 32:27–28). But "Peter" wasn't a nickname; it was a prophecy: "You are . . . You will be." It was as though Jesus said, "You are made of the dust of the earth, but one day you will be a rock." It takes time and a good deal of heat and pressure to produce a solid rock, and it took nearly three years of friendship, prayer, and personal ministry for Jesus to make Peter into a "pillar" and a foundation stone embellished with jewels (Gal. 2:9; Rev. 21:14, 19).

We're so accustomed to finding fault with Peter that we forget that everybody is in the process of becoming. Years ago, it was popular for Christian teens to wear buttons with PBP—GITWMY printed on them. The letters stood for "Please be patient—God isn't through with me yet." We don't wear the buttons today, but we do need the reminder that nobody has "arrived" and all of us are still in process. Peter was impulsive at times (John 18:10–11) and occasionally inconsistent (Matt. 16:13–23), but Jesus helped him overcome those weaknesses to become an effective evangelist and a dynamic leader in the church.

The Bible tells us about many people who accomplished impossible things just because they trusted the Lord and let Him have His way. Moses was wanted for murder in Egypt, but the Lord turned him into history's greatest leader and legislator. Gideon was hiding for his life when the Lord's messenger said to him, "The Lord is with you, mighty warrior" (Judg. 6:12); and he became a mighty warrior!

Nehemiah the king's cupbearer became a fearless leader and builder, and John Mark the runaway became a co-laborer with Paul and even wrote one of the four Gospels. Hebrews 11 summarizes what God can do with ordinary people who will trust Him and obey His instructions.

No, this approach to life isn't a psychological trick ("Thinking will make it so"), nor is it faith in faith ("Just believe!"). Jesus says to each of His children, "You are—you shall be!" But to fulfill that promise, we have to become faithful disciples and let Him do with us what He wants to do.

A New Life

The first miracle Peter experienced was the immediate transformation that occurred when he trusted Jesus Christ and received the gift of eternal life. He described it this way: "Praise be to the God and Father of our Lord Jesus Christ! In his great mercy he has given us new birth into a living hope through the resurrection of Jesus Christ from the dead" (1 Peter 1:3). Life comes from birth, and God's life comes to us through the new birth. We can have a living relationship with the living Christ through the living Word: "For you have been born again, not of perishable seed, but of imperishable, through the living and enduring word of God" (1:23). Peter trusted Jesus, "the living Stone" (2:4), and experienced a new birth that gave him a living hope.

"But that was Peter," we reply defensively. "He was special. He was the rock."

There's no evidence that Peter considered himself different from or superior to anybody else who trusted Christ. He wrote about *all* believers: "You also, like living stones, are being built into a spiritual house" (2:5). My name doesn't mean "rock," but I am a living stone in the temple of God, and so are you if you've trusted Jesus Christ and committed yourself to Him.

Now let's discover how Jesus begins the work of taking ordinary clay and transforming it into rock. Jesus visits Peter's place of employment—the Sea of Galilee—and does a miracle that changes everything.

two

What a Difference a Day Makes

Luke 5:1–11

One day as Jesus was standing by the Lake of Gennesaret, with the people crowding around him and listening to the word of God, he saw at the water's edge two boats, left there by the fishermen, who were washing their nets. He got into one of the boats, the one belonging to Simon, and asked him to put out a little from shore. Then he sat down and taught the people from the boat.

When he had finished speaking, he said to Simon, "Put out into deep water, and let down the nets for a catch."

Simon answered, "Master, we've worked hard all night and haven't caught anything. But because you say so, I will let down the nets."

When they had done so, they caught such a large number of fish that their nets began to break. So they signaled their partners in the other boat to come and help them, and they came and filled both boats so full that they began to sink.

When Simon Peter saw this, he fell at Jesus' knees and said, "Go away from me, Lord; I am a sinful man!" For he and all his companions were astonished at the catch of fish they had taken, and so were James and John, the sons of Zebedee, Simon's partners.

Then Jesus said to Simon, "Don't be afraid; from now on you will catch men." So they pulled their boats up on shore, left everything and followed him.

*A*bove my desk, I keep a small, brittle piece of paper on which is printed a quotation that I clipped out of a newspaper many years ago. It reads: "Make every occasion a great occasion, for you can never tell when somebody may be taking your measure for a larger place [Marsden]." I know nothing about the author, but the quotation has meant a lot to me.

History shows how true this quotation is. Moses was caring for a flock of sheep when God measured him to deliver Israel from Egyptian bondage. God sent a lion and a bear to threaten David's flock when God measured him for the task of killing a giant and ruling a kingdom. Rebekah gave water to a stranger and to his camels and discovered she was being measured to become the wife of Isaac, one of the world's wealthiest men. A young preacher spoke at a Sunday school gathering and so impressed a visitor that he mentioned his name to a friend in London, and that's how

Charles Spurgeon was measured to become pastor of New Park Street Chapel, London.

Peter was about to discover what a difference a day can make! When Jesus stepped into his boat at the Sea of Galilee, Peter didn't realize that he was about to be measured. But as you and I read this familiar story, *we are also being measured.* As we ponder Luke's narrative, we find that we must honestly answer at least four questions, and our answers will tell us how prepared we are to follow Jesus.

Question 1: How Do I Respond to Disappointment and Failure?

Peter and his partners had traveled with Jesus in Galilee and Samaria and had visited Jerusalem with Him at Passover, but their relationship to Him was still somewhat casual. They were learning who He was and what He could do—and perhaps wondering how they would fit in. You get the impression that they occasionally returned home and took care of their work and then returned to be with Jesus. But the day came when Jesus saw they were ready to forsake all and follow Him. It was time for commitment.

New Testament scholars, and people who edit Gospel harmonies, don't agree on how many times Jesus called the four fishermen to become "fishers of men." Some believe that Matthew 4:18–22, Mark 1:16–20, and Luke 5:1–11 all describe the same call, while others see the Luke passage as a separate event—a second call, as it were. But one thing they agree on: Jesus had been rejected in His hometown of Nazareth and had moved His center of ministry to Capernaum, the home of Peter, Andrew, James, and John (Luke 4:16–31). The time had come for the four fishermen to leave everything and follow Jesus.

The four men had fished all night and caught nothing, and now they were preparing their nets so they could go back out and fish some more. I'm neither a fisherman nor a night person, but if I had spent all night fishing and had caught nothing, I wouldn't be preparing my nets—I'd be selling them! But true fishermen aren't quitters, and that may be one reason why Jesus had at least seven fishermen in His disciple band. Peter and his partners had experienced a disappointing night of failure, but that wasn't going to stop them from trying again. They were in the boats mending and cleansing their nets. If nets aren't washed, they tend to collect minute water plants and creatures that can cause rotting; and if nets aren't mended, the tears only get worse. The fishermen couldn't be blamed for not catching any fish, because they worked hard all night, but they could be criticized for not taking good care of their equipment.

Even if you read the Bible casually, you discover that God's people experience failures. Sometimes it's their own fault, and sometimes it's the fault of others, but in the case of Peter and his partners, it was part of the plan of God. Jesus can keep fish out of the nets as easily as He can bring fish into the nets. If Peter had made a good haul the night before, he might have been hesitant to go out again; but his disappointment paved the way for his success. He couldn't control the fish in the sea, but he could control the faith and determination in his own heart. He would learn that success was just a few minutes away.

God has a way of confounding the world and confusing the devil by turning seeming failures into successes for His own glory. Joseph's jealous brothers sold him into slavery, but God made him second ruler of Egypt and preserved the Jewish nation. Elimelech and his family disobeyed God and went to Moab to escape a famine, but Ruth the Moabitess became the great-grandmother of David, Israel's greatest king. Satan used Judas Iscariot to betray Jesus, but Christ's death on the cross defeated Satan and purchased redemption for a lost world. With God, there are no permanent defeats.

Peter passed this first test: He definitely was not a quitter.

Question 2: How Do I Respond to Authority?

Jesus needed a handy "pulpit" from which He could address the vast throng of people on the shore, so He asked Peter to let Him use his boat. Peter was preparing to catch fish, but Jesus was getting Peter ready to fish for people. Our Lord always prepares the way and makes it easier for us to obey His will. As Peter sat in the boat working on his nets, he had to listen to the Lord's message; and when you hear the Word of God, it generates obedient faith (Rom. 10:17).

Peter had faith to invite Jesus into the boat, because all the Master wanted to do was to speak to the crowd. But then Jesus took command of the boat and told Peter, "Put out into deep water, and let down the nets for a catch" (Luke 5:4). What right did Jesus have to control a fisherman's most valuable possession? First Jesus asks for the fishing boat, and now He wants the fishing nets. What will He want next? *He'll want the fisherman!* Jesus was preparing Peter to take the step of faith that will give Him everything so He could start turning clay into rock.

There may have been another question in Peter's mind: What did an unemployed carpenter know about the fishing business? Peter and his fisherman friends knew from experience on the Sea of Galilee that you caught fish in the shallow water in the nighttime, not in the deep water in the daytime. Peter was a well-known fisherman with a reputation to protect, and his friends watching from the shore might laugh at him if he put out into the deep.

The authority of Jesus challenges our training, our expertise, our experience, and even our reputation. But Jesus created the sea Peter's boat sailed on and the fish Peter caught in his nets. He also created the materials from which the boat and the nets had been made. When Jesus asks for our all, He's only asking that we return to Him what He gave us in the first place and what He can manage far better than we can.

In spite of his reservations, Peter called Jesus "Master" and acknowledged His right to give orders and expect obedience. The key to a successful life is found in our obedience to His commands: "But because you say so, I will let down the nets" (v. 5). God honors faith, and faith is revealed by obedience. Faith is simply obeying God in spite of the feelings within us, the circumstances around us, or the consequences before us.

Peter passed the second test: He submitted to Christ's authority and obeyed Him.

Question 3: How Do I Respond to Success?

Peter and Andrew cast the nets into the sea and Jesus filled them with so many fish that the nets began to break. The brothers called to James and John to bring the other boat, and soon both boats were filled with fish and were beginning to sink. The four partners' fellow fishermen standing on shore must have been shocked to see such a large catch taken from the deep water in the daytime.

How did Peter respond to such remarkable success? To begin with, *he shared it with others*. God blesses us so that we might be a blessing to others. "I will bless you," God said to Abraham, "and you will be a blessing" (Gen. 12:2). What we selfishly keep, we ultimately lose; what we generously share, we confidently keep. God keeps the books and knows how to distribute the blessings. It's important that God's servants be more concerned about giving than getting. "It is more blessed to give than to receive" (Acts

20:35), because when you give, you also receive. "Give, and it will be given to you" (Luke 6:38).

There should be no competition in the work of the Lord. The gifts we use for serving Him originally came from His generous hand and so do the blessings that result from our service. When the disciples of John the Baptist reported to John that Jesus was winning more converts than he was, John calmly replied, "A man can receive only what is given him from heaven. . . . He must become greater; I must become less" (John 3:27, 30). The members of the church at Corinth boasted of their spiritual gifts and used them more to show off than to serve, so Paul asked them, "For who makes you different from anyone else? What do you have that you did not receive?" (1 Cor. 4:7).

There was a second response from Peter: *He was humbled by the blessing of God.* How easy it would have been for him to stand in the prow of the ship and shout to the people on shore, "Look at me! I am a successful man!" Instead, he fell at Jesus' knees and said, "Go away from me, Lord; I am a sinful man!" (Luke 5:8). When success humbles you, failure won't crush you. But if success makes you proud, failure will discourage you and perhaps destroy you. More Christian workers have been ruined by success than by failure. After all, when our hearts are right with God, then His goodness and kindness will lead us to repentance (Rom. 2:4). Where there is godly character, success brings humility.

Peter's statement was both right and wrong. Yes, he was a sinner, as all of us are; but no, Jesus had no plans to depart. His plan was just the opposite: He was about to call Peter and his partners to follow Him and be with Him to the very end. Peter has been called impetuous, and at times the description fits; but no matter what Peter said or did, he was trying to say something that was difficult for him to express. There in the ship, he felt his unworthiness even to be with Jesus, let alone receive His bounty. He had the right attitude but spoke the wrong words, and perhaps you and I have committed the same sin.

It's remarkable how many "great people" in Scripture have confessed their unworthiness to the Lord. Abraham called himself "dust and ashes" (Gen. 18:27); and Jacob, the father of the twelve tribes of Israel, said, "I am unworthy of all the kindness and faithfulness you have shown your servant" (32:10). King David prayed, "Who am I, O Sovereign LORD, and what is my family, that you have brought me this far?" (2 Sam. 7:18). Job said to the Lord, "Therefore I despise myself and repent in dust and ashes" (Job 42:6). The apostle Paul wrote, "Christ Jesus came into the world to save sinners—of whom I am the worst" (1 Tim. 1:15), and he considered himself "less than the least of all God's people" (Eph. 3:8). Where does this leave the rest of us?

Some people only *swell* when they are especially blessed of God, but Peter *grew*. God gave him great success, and he didn't become proud or take credit for what happened. He said to himself, "I'm not worthy of this kind of blessing. I know my sinful heart, and if this happens too often, I may get proud. I need the Lord's help!" When God has richly blessed you, the safest place to be is at the feet of Jesus.

Peter passed the third test: He knew how to handle success.

Question 4: How Do I Respond to the Life of Faith?

"Do not be afraid" is a statement found seven times in the Gospel of Luke (1:13, 30; 2:10; 5:10; 8:50; 12:7, 32), but what was there for Peter to fear? For one thing, this one miracle had wiped out all of his training and past experience, and Peter had to start life all over again as if he knew nothing about boats and fishing. That could unnerve a man. Most adults find their identity and worth in their vocation, whether they are teaching school, raising a family, driving a truck, or performing surgery. Christians don't "have jobs," they have "vocations," which means "callings." They are called by God to fulfill certain purposes in this world. Peter was called to be a fisherman, but now he was convinced that he really didn't know much about fishing.

All his years as a fisherman weren't wasted, though, because God never wastes anything. Jesus called Peter and his partners to become "fishers of men." Jesus didn't invent that phrase; it had been around for a long time. Greek philosophers and Jewish rabbis used this image to describe "catching disciples by casting out the net of truth." The four fishermen had been catching living fish in their nets, but then the fish died; now they would catch dead fish— dead sinners—in the "gospel net," and these fish would receive life! The same courage, tenacity, cooperation, and wisdom that had made them good fishermen would help make them good evangelists.

Jesus called them to a life of faith. The four men signed their names to a blank piece of paper, as it were, and Jesus wrote the contract without asking for their counsel. You either reject or accept the will of God; you never negotiate it. The life of faith means following Jesus, and that means He goes before us and prepares the way. He also prepares the workers for the work (Eph. 2:10) and enables them to do each assignment (Phil. 2:12–13). The life of faith isn't a "leap into the dark," because we're following Him who is the Light of the world (John 8:12). We're guided by the Word of God which is a lamp to our feet and a light to our path (Ps. 119:105).

In that day, Jewish rabbis didn't call their disciples; they waited for the disciples to come to them and ask for the privilege of learning from them. Jesus, however, calls all of God's people to follow Him and find a life of purpose and fulfillment. It isn't an experience of "making a living" but "making a life." There are no "self-made people" in the ranks of Christ's disciples, because our Lord's promise is, "I will make you." The apostle Paul was a gifted and well-trained man, but he openly confessed, "But by the grace of God I am what I am" (1 Cor. 15:10).

Peter passed the fourth test: He left everything and followed Christ.

three

Miracles Can Happen at Home

Matthew 8:14–17; Mark 1:21–34; Luke 4:31–41

When Jesus came into Peter's house, he saw Peter's mother-in-law lying in bed with a fever. He touched her hand and the fever left her, and she got up and began to wait on him.

When evening came, many who were demon-possessed were brought to him, and he drove out the spirits with a word and healed all the sick. This was to fulfill what was spoken through the prophet Isaiah:
>"He took up our infirmities
>and carried our diseases."

Matthew 8:14–17

A London newspaper sponsored a contest for the best definition of *home*, and the winning entry was, "Home is the place where we are treated the best and complain the most." The American poet Robert Frost called home "the place where, when you have to go there, They have to take you in";[1] but the American humorist Elbert Hubbard said that home was "the place where we go to change our clothes so as to go somewhere else." Perhaps all three definitions are true at different times in our lives. I think the British essayist Samuel Johnson said it best: "That's the part of the world where people know when you're sick, miss you when you die, and love you while you live."

A miracle took place in Peter's home in Capernaum, and it encourages us to heed some practical admonitions if we want to see the Lord bless our own homes as well.

Let's Invite Jesus into Our Homes

Peter, Andrew, James, and John attended the Sabbath service with Jesus at the synagogue in Capernaum, and there they had seen Him deliver a man from demonic bondage (Mark 1:21–28). After the service, Peter invited Jesus to go home with them and enjoy the day. The weekly Sabbath dinner was a very special meal, and Peter wanted to share it with the Master. Peter was married (1 Cor. 9:5), and in the home were Peter and his wife, his brother Andrew, and his wife's mother. It's likely that Jesus made Peter's home His headquarters whenever He was in Capernaum and that Peter's roof was the one torn up so the paralytic could be brought to Jesus for healing (Luke 5:17–26).

Unlike John the Baptist, who didn't mingle with people socially, Jesus accepted dinner invitations and was even accused of being a glutton and a drunkard (Matt. 11:19). He attended a marriage celebration at Cana (John 2),

He dined with Levi (Matthew) so He could meet his "sinner" friends (Matt. 9:9–13), and He even ate with His enemies who were always trying to trap Him (Luke 14:1–14). Jesus used these social events as opportunities for telling people about the Father and the blessings of the kingdom (see 1 Cor. 10:31).

Years ago, many Christian people hung a motto in their homes that told visitors that Jesus Christ was a member of the family. It said:

> Jesus Christ is the Head of this home,
> The unseen Guest at every meal,
> The silent Listener to every conversation.

Peter didn't have this motto hanging on the wall in his house, but he did have the Master in his home, and that was even better. Not only should we invite Jesus into our hearts and (if we marry) to our wedding, but we should also welcome the Lord into each place where we live; for God is our true and lasting abode: "Lord, you have been our dwelling place throughout all generations" (Ps. 90:1). The believer's permanent address is always "in Christ." As Jesus said, "If anyone loves me, he will obey my teaching. My Father will love him, and we will come to him and make our home with him" (John 14:23).

Making Jesus the Head of the home involves much more than putting an attractive motto on the wall. It means making Him Lord of our lives, listening daily to His Word, and seeking to glorify Him in the affairs of the home. It means keeping out anything that would grieve Him and welcoming everything that will honor Him. A truly Christian home isn't odd or eccentric, but it is different, and visitors should be able to detect the difference. It's a place where Jesus Christ is worshiped and served seven days a week and where every person and resource is always at His disposal.

Let's Tell Jesus Our Needs

When Jesus and the four disciples entered Peter's home, they found that his mother-in-law was sick in bed with a fever (Mark 1:29–30). We don't know what her sickness was, but we do know that it produced a high fever that nothing could relieve. High fevers make you sweat profusely and ache all over, and no matter what position you take in your bed, you're always uncomfortable. You toss and turn and try to sleep, but you're miserable no matter what you do. Today we have medicines that will break fevers like that, but in Jesus' day, all that the patient could do was suffer and wait it out.

Peter had only recently responded to Christ's call to follow Him, and already he was facing a crisis in his own home and family. He was learning quickly that devotion to Christ doesn't guarantee we'll be sheltered from the normal problems and cares of life. In fact, Peter would later write, "Cast all your anxiety on him because he cares for you" (1 Peter 5:7). Before his life ended, Peter would have personally tested and proved the promise of Psalm 55:22: "Cast your cares on the Lord and he will sustain you." He experienced the power of Christ in his life every day.

The four disciples had seen Jesus do a mighty miracle in the synagogue that morning when He cast the demon out of a man (Mark 1:21–28), so surely He could reveal His power in Peter's humble home. It's one thing to go to church and worship God with great devotion, surrounded by enthusiastic people, but it is quite something else to go home and trust Him to do His mighty works there. Truly, the real test of our devotion and faith isn't what happens in the glare of the public meeting but what happens in the privacy of our own home. Peter's faith had worked on the Sea of Galilee, so why shouldn't it work now?

Matthew focuses on Jesus seeing Peter's mother-in-law lying sick in bed (Matt. 8:14). Mark and Luke, however, add the element of the disciples' intercession on her behalf. Mark reports that the men told Jesus about her need (Mark 1:30), and Luke wrote that "they asked Jesus to help her." (Luke 4:38). Jesus, in turn, answered their request and healed Peter's mother-in-law (Matt. 8:15; Mark 1:31; Luke 4:39).

This story teaches us that even though the Lord sees and knows our needs, we still need to pray, because prayer is one of God's appointed means for meeting our needs (see James 4:2). Prayer is essential if we want to see the power of God work in our own lives and in the lives of those we care about. Prayer is also something we need to grow in. We never graduate from the school of prayer, but that doesn't mean we should remain in kindergarten! Prayer means much more than telling God our needs and asking for His help. It also involves developing a closer relationship with the Father and the Son through the Spirit's ministry. As we grow in our prayer life, we come to understand God's will better and know what to pray for and how to ask when we don't know. It also means making ourselves available to be a part of the answer if God calls us to act, because God wants to work through us as well as for us (Eph. 3:20). True intercessors are always willing to do the will of God.

Let's Trust Jesus to Work

Faith and prayer go together; otherwise prayer is only a meaningless religious ritual. As Jesus promised His disciples, "Therefore I tell you, whatever you ask for in prayer, believe that you have received it, and it will be yours" (Mark 11:24). In the weeks to come, Peter and his friends would discover that they could trust Jesus with any problem at any time and in any place. Nothing is too hard for Him.

Jesus entered Peter's house as a Sabbath Day guest, but He soon became the Master of the house and took charge, just as He had taken charge of Peter's boat. When we let Jesus take charge, wonderful things begin to happen. Jesus went to the woman, stood over her, stooped and took her by the hand. He rebuked the fever and lifted the woman up, and she was completely delivered from her sickness. There was no need for her to convalesce because His power had imparted instant health to her body.

God doesn't always grant instant health in response to believing prayer; sometimes He uses and blesses the means provided by the medical profession. With or without means, healing is still the gift of God. I heard one physician say, "I send the bill, but it's God who does the healing." The Scottish novelist George Macdonald has pointed out that our Lord's miracles achieved instantly what the Father is always doing gradually. The Father is always multiplying grain, season by season; but Jesus multiplied the bread instantly. Season by season, the Father is turning water into wine, but Jesus did it instantly at the wedding feast. Either way, it is God who is at work.

We also need to face the fact that God doesn't always see fit to heal everybody for whom we pray. All the people Jesus healed, and even those He raised from the dead, eventually died from one cause or another because nobody lives forever in this mortal body. In my pastoral ministry, I've joined God's people in praying for the sick and afflicted, and not all of them were healed. No matter what the result, though, we need to say with Job, "The LORD gave and the LORD has taken away; may the name of the LORD be praised" (Job 1:21).

Jesus Christ is certainly the Great Physician (Matt. 9:12), and He even makes house calls! When He diagnoses the case, He's always accurate. His cures are complete and final—and He pays the bill!

Let's Show Jesus Our Gratitude

Peter's mother-in-law immediately waited on Jesus and the four disciples, helping serve the Sabbath meal (Matt. 8:15; Mark 1:31; Luke 4:39). This was her way of thanking Him for what He had done for her. There's no evidence that she volunteered to be a missionary or asked Jesus for some special ministry. She simply went back to her old responsibilities with a heart full of love and gratitude, and this transformed the old tasks into new opportunities to please Jesus. Like Mary's ministry to Jesus in Bethany (John 12:1–3), what Peter's wife's mother did was seen by very few people, but it has become a blessing to the whole world.

During His earthly ministry, Jesus healed multitudes. Not all of them became faithful disciples, though, and at least one of them turned state's evidence against Jesus (John 5:1–15). When their loved ones were healed or their bodies were fed, too many people were grateful for the gift but forgot the Giver. Not so in Peter's house! Peter's mother-in-law immediately did what she could to serve the Lord and please Him.

Jesus ate the Sabbath meal and no doubt rested, and it's a good thing He did, because He was about to enter into a demanding evening of ministry. Because of the miracle He had performed in the synagogue that morning, the word spread that He was in the neighborhood (Mark 1:28; Luke 4:37). When the Sabbath ended, the Jews brought sick and demonized people to Peter's house, and the whole city gathered at the door! Though Jesus paid no attention to man-made rules, it was against the Jewish tradition to heal on the Sabbath, so the crowd waited until sundown. (There were thirty-nine kinds of work prohibited on the Sabbath, and healing the sick was one of them.) Jesus spoke the word and the demons fled. He laid hands on the afflicted and they were healed. Nobody was rejected, and nobody went home in the same condition he or she had come. He healed them all.

When Jesus is invited into a home, that home should become a source of blessing to the community; because when Jesus is Lord, you want to share Him with others. What every neighborhood needs is a vibrant Christian home like that of Peter and his wife. If our discipleship doesn't begin at home, it's not likely to accomplish much anyplace else. The four men had gone to the synagogue with Jesus, and then Peter had invited Him to go home with them. From this small beginning, great blessings came to many people.

When Matthew wrote his account of Christ healing the crowds at Peter's house, he saw in it the fulfillment of Isaiah's prophecy: "He took up our infirmities and carried our diseases" (Matt. 8:17; see Isa. 53:4). Some have interpreted this to mean that there is "healing in the atonement," and that every believer can claim physical healing and receive it. But Matthew wrote about Jesus taking human affliction *during His ministry on earth,* not on the cross. To be sure, our Lord's sacrificial death on the cross is the basis for every blessing we enjoy. One day each believer will have a glorified body because Jesus died for us, but we don't have it now nor can we "claim it" now. In Scripture, the healing of sickness is a picture of salvation (Ps. 103:3; Matt. 9:1–8); when Peter quoted Isaiah 53:4, he applied it that way (1 Peter 2:24).

Most of our Lord's miracles were performed before crowds in public, but this is the first of six recorded miracles that Jesus performed in homes. He healed a paralytic, probably in Peter's home (Mark 2:1–12), the nobleman's son (John 4:43–54), the centurion's servant (Luke 7:1–10), and the daughter of the Canaanite woman (Matt. 15:21–28). In the home of Jairus, Jesus raised his twelve-year-old daughter from the dead (Mark 5:21–43).

Our Lord can still do the miraculous in our homes if we'll invite Him in and let Him be the Head of the house.

four

A STATEMENT OF FAITH
FOR STORMY NIGHTS

Matthew 14:22–36; Mark 6:45–56; John 6:15–21

Immediately Jesus made the disciples get into the boat and go on ahead of him to the other side, while he dismissed the crowd. After he had dismissed them, he went up on a mountainside by himself to pray. When evening came, he was there alone, but the boat was already a considerable distance from land, buffeted by the waves because the wind was against it.

During the fourth watch of the night Jesus went out to them, walking on the lake. When the disciples saw him walking on the lake, they were terrified. "It's a ghost," they said, and cried out in fear.

But Jesus immediately said to them: "Take courage! It is I. Don't be afraid."

"Lord, if it's you," Peter replied, "tell me to come to you on the water."

"Come," he said.

Then Peter got down out of the boat, walked on the water and came toward Jesus. But when he saw the wind, he was afraid and, beginning to sink, cried out, "Lord, save me!"

Immediately Jesus reached out his hand and caught him. "You of little faith," he said, "why did you doubt?"

Matthew 14:22–31

*O*n April 23, 1834, the American essayist Ralph Waldo Emerson wrote in his journal, "Rain. Rain. The good rain, like a bad preacher, does not know when to leave off." A few years later, his friend Henry Wadsworth Longfellow would watch an autumn storm and see in it the image of his vanished youth and his impending old age, days that would be "dark and dreary." But he rallied his faith and wrote in the last verse:

> Be still, sad heart! and cease repining;
> Behind the clouds is the sun still shining:
> Thy fate is the common fate of all:
> Into each life some rain must fall,
> Some days must be dark and dreary.

Or as our Arab friends express it, "All sunshine makes a desert."

I happen to like rainy days, especially if I can stay indoors. It's the perfect time to drink tea, read a good book, and listen to music. But I also enjoy walking in the rain (if I'm adequately covered), because the different atmosphere quickens my mind and heart and helps me get a new perspective on different aspects of life. When I was a boy, I often sat on our front porch during rainstorms. All I did was watch the rain and ponder things in general and nothing in particular.

However, I remember one boyhood storm that really frightened me. I was in a boat on Sturgeon Bay, Wisconsin, with my father, my two brothers, and my Uncle Roy; and we were out at the reef fishing. It was early evening and the fish were biting so enthusiastically that we didn't even put our catches on the stringer—we just threw them in the bottom of the boat.

"There's a storm coming," Uncle Roy said suddenly. He was very wise in matters related to water, weather, and fishing, especially on Sturgeon Bay. "We'd better head for shore right now."

We pulled in our lines and my big brother started the motor; but the storm had a head start and reached the shore before we did. By the time we docked, we were thoroughly soaked, and I was thoroughly scared. The only passengers on the trip that enjoyed the pelting rain were the fish flopping in the bottom of the boat, but they didn't know what lay ahead of them.

I wouldn't have wanted to be with the disciples when they were caught in a storm one night on the Sea of Galilee. The storm was much greater than the one I just described, and they didn't have a motor on their boat. They felt the fierce wind blowing against them, and they strained at the oars so the boat wouldn't be driven against the rocks on shore. The one time I was in a boat on the Sea of Galilee was on a warm sunny day, and our tour group was heading for Capernaum. I shouted to our guide, "Have you ever been in a storm on these waters?" His face clouded. "Yes," he called, "and I don't want to go through it again!"

Storms do come to our lives, though, and we have to be prepared. It's one thing to have wet clothes and cold skin, both of which can be remedied, but it's quite something else to have a broken heart and a shattered life and be left floundering in the sea of life with no hope. What life does to us depends a great deal on what life finds in us, and what those disciples needed was faith. So do we. Let me suggest a "statement of faith" that will encourage us in the storms of life. It contains five simple affirmations.

He Brought Me Here

Some storms we cause ourselves because we disobey the Lord. Jonah is a good example of this. So is King David after his adultery with Bathsheba, though his "storm" hit him on land and not on the water. Some storms are like the one described in Acts 27—they come because others disobey God and we happen to be on board. Paul warned the Roman centurion that trouble was coming, but the officer preferred to listen to the "experts," call for a vote, and then take advantage of the south wind that was blowing softly. That south wind soon became a stormy wind, and everything was lost except the passengers and the boards on which they paddled to shore. The storm wasn't Paul's fault, but he still suffered.

The disciples, however, were in a storm *because they obeyed the Master!* Knowing full well that a storm was coming, Jesus sent the men across the lake (Matt. 14:22–24). They had just assisted Him in feeding more than five thousand people (14:13–21), and if any thirteen men were popular, it was Jesus and His disciples. The crowd was so excited about their miraculous free meal that they wanted to make Jesus king, and the disciples were enthusiastic about their plan. Peter would have become prime minister, Judas would be the treasurer, and the other disciples the members of Jesus' court. The Master knew the danger of this kind of thinking, so He compelled the men to get into the boat and go to the other shore. That command in itself should have assured them that they would reach their destination, but the men seemed to forget it when the storm threatened their lives.

As I look back at my own life and ministry, I see that God has used two different kinds of storms to guide me. *Correcting storms* come to chasten us when we've disobeyed God's will, but *perfecting storms* come because we've obeyed the Lord. I recall when my wife and I were serving our first church and planning to go to the mission field. We were expecting our first child when Betty came down with the mumps. The doctor confined her to bed for the duration of the sickness, and the day she was allowed to get up, I slipped on the ice and fractured my right ankle! I wasn't able to leave home and had to forego my weekly trip to Roosevelt University in Chicago where I was doing graduate work in preparation for missionary appointment. During those weeks of recuperation, the Lord spoke to both of us about our ministry plans and made it clear that we were to stay home and pastor churches, not go to the mission field. Disappointment? Yes, but as A. T. Pierson used to say, "Disappointment—His appointment."

If the storm you are in is a correcting storm, settle accounts with the Lord and get back on the right track. If it's a perfecting storm, wait on the Lord and trust Him to see you through. No matter how difficult the storm may be, it's much easier to endure the storm than to feel the pain that comes when we get out of the will of God. Furthermore, in the storm the Lord will prepare you for what He's preparing for you. The disciples would face many storms of trial and persecution during their service for the Lord, and they needed to know that the obedient heart never has to fear the wind or the waves.

While we were serving that first church, the Lord led us to construct a new sanctuary, which was desperately needed. I couldn't build a birdhouse from a kit, let alone direct the construction of a church, but the Lord chooses the foolish things of the world to confound the mighty. There were the usual delays, and by the time the wooden arches were in place, it was winter and construction ceased. During my pastoral rounds, when I drove past the building site and saw those beautiful arches covered with ice and snow, I almost developed ulcers. Then the Lord showed me Psalm 148:8, "Lightning and hail, snow and clouds, stormy winds that do his bidding." Whether God sends a correcting storm or a perfecting storm, we have nothing to fear, because He's accomplishing His will.

He Is Praying for Me

After Jesus compelled His disciples to get into the boat and leave, He Himself went alone and prayed (Matt. 14:23). No doubt the disciples looked back and saw Him going up the mountainside, and they knew what He was doing. They had learned that after He ministered to the crowds, Jesus often went off by Himself so He could meditate and pray. They knew that He would include them in His prayers, and that His prayers were always answered. We neither see Him nor hear Him, but our Lord is now in heaven "at the right hand of God and is also interceding for us" (Rom. 8:34). He always lives to intercede for His people (Heb. 7:25).

This is one of two vivid pictures in Scripture of our Lord's intercessory ministry. Jesus is on the mountain and looks through the storm and sees the plight of the disciples in the boat. "He saw the disciples straining at the oars" (Mark 6:48). He felt their burdens and entered sympathetically into their struggle (Heb. 4:14–16). Satan would have drowned them, but the prayers of the Savior kept them safe.

The second picture is in Exodus 17:8–15, where Moses stood on the top of the hill and helped Joshua fight the Amalekites down in the valley. As long as Moses held his hands up, Joshua and his soldiers got the upper hand, but when Moses dropped his hands, the Amalekites started to win. Aaron and Hur held up Moses' arms until Joshua defeated the enemy. Of course, our heavenly Intercessor needs no help to win any battle, because on the cross He already defeated every enemy. We don't fight *for* victory but *from* victory, and our responsibility is to come to the throne of grace and ask for the grace and mercy that we need. Knowing that He is praying for us encourages us as we pray to Him.

It's easy to feel lonely in the storms of life and wonder if anybody really cares. "Look to my right and see; no one is concerned for me," said David in an hour of despair. "I have no refuge; no one cares for my life." Then he cried out to God in a burst of faith, "You are my refuge, my portion in the land of the living" (Ps. 142:4–5). We are prone to look back and thank God for Calvary where Jesus died for us and to look ahead and anticipate the time when Jesus will come for us. But we also need to look up and remind ourselves that Jesus is living for us and interceding for us. The enemy wants us to feel like we're alone and abandoned, but Jesus promised never to leave us or forsake us (Matt. 28:20; Heb. 13:5).

He Will Come to Me

The Lord is always with us, but sometimes He comes to us in a special way and reveals Himself to us. In the darkest hour of the night, when the disciples were perhaps ready to give up, He came to them walking on the water. The waves that frightened them were only stairsteps for the Master to come to His beloved disciples and rescue them. "When you pass through the waters, I will be with you; and when you pass through the rivers, they will not sweep over you" (Isa. 43:2).

You can walk through the picture gallery of Scripture and meet many people who knew what it meant to have the assurance of the presence of the Lord during their hours of pain and difficulty. "The LORD was with Joseph. . . . But while Joseph was there in the prison, the LORD was with him. . . . The LORD was with Joseph and gave him success in whatever he did" (Gen. 39:2, 20–21, 23). Joshua met Jesus at Jericho, where the Lord presented Himself as a conquering general (Josh. 5:13–15)—He always comes to us in a form that encourages us. He walked in the furnace with the three faithful Jewish men (Dan. 3:24–25), and He stood with Paul in Corinth (Acts 18:9–10), Jerusalem (23:11), and in the storm (27:22–24). During Paul's trial before Caesar, the believers in Rome abandoned him, but the Lord stood with him (2 Tim. 4:16–17).

The trouble is, we don't always recognize Jesus when He does come. The disciples thought that the figure walking on the waves was a ghost, and the last thing they needed was an apparition from the world of the dead! Mark tells us that Jesus was about to walk past them when they cried out in fear (Mark 6:48). But if He came to assure them and to rescue them, why walk past them? Was He waiting for them to recognize Him and invite Him into the boat, or was He only testing their faith? Some translate the text "for He intended to pass their way." One thing is sure: The sound of His voice and the assurance of His word brought confidence to the frightened men, which reminds us that we too need to hear His Word when we find ourselves in the storms of life.

When God's people finally arrive in heaven, perhaps the Lord will host "This Is Your Life" and show each of us how many times Jesus was with us and we didn't recognize Him. Total strangers who were on hand when we desperately needed help may turn out to have been His angels in disguise. The day of miracles isn't ended, and the Lord still takes care of His own.

He Will Help Me Grow

One of the purposes of storms is to help us "grow in the grace and knowledge of our Lord and Savior Jesus Christ" (2 Peter 3:18). We mature in our faith, not by listening to weather reports, but by going through the storm. "And the God of all grace, who called you to his eternal glory in Christ, after you have suffered a little while, will himself restore you and make you strong, firm and steadfast" (1 Peter 5:10). That sounds like the description of a rock—strong, firm, and steadfast.

Peter was a fisherman, so the Lord used experiences with boats, nets, and storms to encourage him to grow. The first lesson occurred on a clear day when the Sea of Galilee was calm (Luke 5:1–11). First, Jesus asked Peter to thrust out a little from the land so He could use the boat for a "pulpit" and teach the people standing on the shore. When the sermon was over, Jesus commanded Peter to launch out into the deep water, and there he caught so many fish that his nets began to break and he had to call his partners for help. If you had asked Peter, "What did you learn today?" he would have replied, "I learned that I can trust Jesus to care for me on clear days when the sea is calm."

The next lesson took place at night when the sea was stormy and Jesus was asleep in the boat (Matt. 8:23–27). The frightened disciples were so sure this was the end that they awakened Jesus with their cries, "Lord, save us! We're going to drown!" (v. 25). He stood and rebuked the storm, and a great calm came over the sea. What did Peter learn? That he could trust Christ at night, in the storm, even when He was asleep in the boat.

The third lesson was even greater, because Peter learned that he could trust Christ at night in the storm when Jesus wasn't even in the boat! In fact, Peter learned that he could depend on Jesus *even without a boat,* for he got out of the boat and walked on the water! All Jesus said to him was "Come!" and on the strength of that one word, Peter did the impossible (Matt. 14:28–29).

Yes, Peter began to sink, but he *knew* he was sinking, and he had the faith to cry out to Jesus for help (v. 30). The other disciples weren't sinking, not because they had more faith than Peter, but because they were still in the boat. Before we criticize Peter, let's look at ourselves and honestly examine our own faith and courage. It was Peter's love for Jesus that drew him out of the boat to go to the Master, and it was his faith in Jesus that saved him from drowning in waters that were very familiar to him. Peter dared to be different, and that's the kind of follower Jesus wants to call.

Why did Peter begin to sink? Because he saw the waves and felt the wind and began to waver in his faith. He was distracted from watching Jesus because of the circumstances around him, something all of us have done at one time or another. We can't successfully walk on the waves or run the race unless by faith we "fix our eyes on Jesus" (Heb. 12:2). Circumstances are those nasty things we see when we stop looking to Jesus in the Word and claiming His promises. Our Lord's one word "Come!" was enough for Peter to lay hold of and be enabled to participate in a miracle.

Earlier, when Peter hauled in that great catch of fish described in Luke 5, he got distracted and began to look at himself: "Go away from me, Lord; I am a sinful man!" (Luke 5:8). Suppose Jesus had answered that prayer? What would have happened to Peter and his three partners? It isn't wrong for us to examine our hearts and honestly confess our sins, but it is wrong to do so without looking by faith to Jesus. Without faith in Jesus, self-examination brings despair; but with Jesus, it brings cleansing and a new beginning.

There's a third time when Peter was distracted: when Jesus restored him to his discipleship and said, "Follow me!" (John 21:15–23). Peter began to follow Christ, but then he heard footsteps behind him and turned to find John also following. Peter asked, "Lord, what about him?" *Peter got his eyes off of Christ and began to look at other believers.* Jesus rebuked him for doing this and repeated His call: "You must follow me" (v. 22).

If we look to Jesus by faith, we can do whatever He commands us to do. But if we start looking at ourselves, our circumstances, or at other believers, we'll start to stumble, fall, and sink. The only way to be an overcomer is to exercise faith in the Lord (1 John 5:4). Peter was an overcomer; he walked back to the ship with Jesus!

He Will See Me Through

The disciples in the boat had already seen three miracles: Jesus walking on the water, Peter walking on the water, and Peter being rescued from drowning. But when Jesus and Peter got into the boat, two more miracles occurred: The storm ceased, and the boat instantly arrived at its destination on the other shore (Mark 6:51; John 6:21). No wonder the men fell before Jesus and worshiped Him, calling Him the Son of God. When He had calmed the storm described in Matthew 8:23–27, the men had asked, "What kind of man is this?" (Matt. 8:27). But now their question marks had become exclamation points: "Truly you are the Son of God" (Matt. 14:33).

Jesus is the "author and perfecter of our faith" (Heb. 12:2), which means that whatever He starts, He finishes. Abraham, Isaac, and Jacob weren't perfect men, but the Lord kept His promises to them and fulfilled His promises in them and through them because they walked with Him by faith. Abraham became the father of a son, Isaac, and Isaac the father of Jacob and Esau. The Lord said to Jacob, when he was fleeing from home, "I will not leave you until I have done what I have promised you" (Gen. 28:15). And He kept all His promises.

The life of faith isn't always easy, but the life of doubt and unbelief is much harder. "The LORD will fulfill his purpose for me," wrote David (Ps. 138:8), and Paul wrote, "Being confident of this, that he who began a good work in you will carry it on to completion until the day of Christ Jesus" (Phil. 1:6).

He will see you through!

The British preacher and composer John Newton said it perfectly:

> Be gone, unbelief;
> My Savior is near,
> And for my relief
> Will surely appear;
> By prayer let me wrestle
> And He will perform;
> With Christ in the vessel,
> I smile at the storm.

five

THE KINGDOM AND THE GLORY

Matthew 16:21–17:23; Luke 9:27–45

About eight days after Jesus said this, he took Peter, John and James with him and went up onto a mountain to pray. As he was praying, the appearance of his face changed, and his clothes became as bright as a flash of lightning. Two men, Moses and Elijah, appeared in glorious splendor, talking with Jesus. They spoke about his departure, which he was about to bring to fulfillment at Jerusalem. Peter and his companions were very sleepy, but when they became fully awake, they saw his glory and the two men standing with him. As the men were leaving Jesus, Peter said to him,

"Master, it is good for us to be here. Let us put up three shelters—one for you, one for Moses and one for Elijah." (He did not know what he was saying.)

While he was speaking, a cloud appeared and enveloped them, and they were afraid as they entered the cloud. A voice came from the cloud, saying, "This is my Son, whom I have chosen; listen to him." When the voice had spoken, they found that Jesus was alone. The disciples kept this to themselves, and told no one at that time what they had seen.

Luke 9:28–36

*W*hen Jesus first confided to His disciples that He was going to Jerusalem to be rejected and crucified, Peter immediately opposed the plan. "Never, Lord!" was his response. "This shall never happen to you!" (Matt. 16:22). As far as the record is concerned, the other disciples said nothing, but they probably agreed with Peter. Their focus was on an earthly Jewish kingdom and the restoration of David's throne. Jesus publicly rebuked Peter for opposing the Father's will, because Peter was thinking like the unbelieving world and acting like the enemy. The Lord then gave the Twelve a short sermon on discipleship and cross-bearing, and then He added a promise: "I tell you the truth, some who are standing here will not taste death before they see the Son of Man coming in his kingdom" (16:28).

About a week later, Peter, James, and John went to the mount with Jesus and saw His glory. Years later, Peter wrote about this experience: "We were eyewitnesses of his majesty. . . . We ourselves heard this voice that came from heaven when we were with him on the sacred mountain" (2 Peter 1:16, 18). What Peter and his two friends saw and heard on the mount conveys to believers today some basic truths that help us understand and experience our own personal transfigurations.

Jesus Christ Is God's Son

The disciples had seen Jesus perform marvelous deeds that revealed the glory of God (John 2:11), but this was the first time they had actually beheld that glory radiating through His being. He had veiled His glory in human flesh, but now His countenance and clothing were radiant and so was the cloud that came down and covered them. Peter had confessed, "You are the Christ, the Son of the living God" (Matt. 16:16), and now that witness was verified and strengthened by the manifestation of His glory. That's the usual biblical order: first faith, then sight: "Did I not tell you that if you believed, you would see the glory of God?" (John 11:40).

The apostle John wrote, "We have seen his glory, the glory of the One and Only, who came from the Father, full of grace and truth" (John 1:14). We didn't have that privilege, but we know that one day we shall see Him and be like Him in His glory (1 John 3:1–3). Jesus will "transform our lowly bodies so that they will be like his glorious body" (Phil. 3:21).

Moses and Elijah were with Christ on the mount, and Moses had seen the glory of God descend from heaven and rest in the Holy of Holies in the tabernacle (Exod. 40:34–35). The pillar of cloud guided the Israelites as they journeyed, and it rested over the tabernacle when the people camped. Moses had beheld the glory of God on Mount Sinai when he received the law, and on more than one occasion he had seen God's glory appear in the camp of Israel and execute judgment against rebellious people.

It's a serious thing to behold the glory of God; the manifestation of God's glory is an awesome event that transcends anything that humans can do. All of our glory is like the flowers of the field, here today and gone tomorrow (Isa.

40:6–7). The glory of reputation is blasted by scandal, the glory of riches is destroyed by a change in the stock market, and all human glory is wiped out by death. But the glory of the Lord abides forever.

In this day of contrived images, manufactured fame, and cheap tinsel substitutes for the glory that only the Lord can give, it does us good to contemplate the glory of Jesus Christ and get in touch with reality. At His birth, the glory of God provided the perfect setting for the announcement the angels brought (Luke 2:8–14), and during His life, Jesus glorified the Father by always doing His perfect will (John 8:29). Even His shameful death as a criminal on a Roman cross brought glory to God. "The hour has come for the Son of Man to be glorified" is the way Jesus expressed it (John 12:23). We would have used the word *crucified*, but Jesus looked beyond the cross to "the joy set before him" (Heb. 12:2). In all that Jesus is, all He does, and all He says, our Lord expresses the glory of God, for "the Son is the radiance of God's glory and the exact representation of his being" (Heb. 1:3).

Something else, however, proves to us that Jesus is the Son of God: The Father spoke from heaven and said, "This is my son, whom I love; with him I am well pleased" (Matt. 17:5; see also 2 Peter 1:17). The Father had spoken similar words at the baptism of Jesus (Matt. 3:17), and Satan referred to this statement when he tempted our Lord in the wilderness: "If you are the Son of God, tell these stones to become bread" (Matt. 4:3). The Father declared His love for the Son, *yet the Son was hungry!* The Father declared His love for His Son, *yet the Son would die on a cross!* "Jesus loved Martha and her sister and Lazarus" (John 11:5), *yet Jesus delayed so long in going to Bethany that Lazarus died!* The love of God for us is no guarantee that we'll always enjoy comfortable circumstances and never experience trials and tears. No matter what we see around us or feel within us, God loves us and His love will never change.

God's Kingdom Will Come

Peter protested against Jesus going to the cross because he was a loyal Jew who believed the Old Testament prophecies about Israel's future glorious kingdom. If Jesus truly was the Messiah, as Peter confessed, then He would defeat His enemies and not be defeated by them. He would restore the fallen throne and scepter of David and usher in a new age of peace, prosperity, and spiritual blessing for Israel, the kingdom described by prophets and psalmists in the Old Testament Scriptures.

Jesus didn't deny that the kingdom prophecies would be fulfilled. In fact, He did just the opposite and demonstrated the certainty and the glory of the future kingdom. He had promised that Peter, James, and John would "see the Son of Man coming in his kingdom" (Matt. 16:28), and He kept His promise. Moses and Elijah represented the Old Testament saints as well as the Law and the Prophets, and the three apostles represented the New Testament saints—and all of them shared the glory. What Peter and his friends needed to learn was that this promised kingdom could come only through the suffering and death of the King.

One reason Peter wrote his second epistle was to refute the false teachers who questioned and denied the coming kingdom of Christ, asking, "Where is this 'coming' he promised?" (2 Peter 3:4). As far as these blind leaders were concerned, it was futile for God's people to pray "Thy kingdom come" because the request would not be granted. But Jesus *will* come again and His righteous kingdom *will* be established on earth! One day the loud voices from heaven will announce, "The kingdom of the world has become the kingdom of our Lord and of his Christ, and he will reign for ever and ever" (Rev. 11:15).

What difference does it make in our lives today if we eagerly expect the return of Jesus Christ and the establishment of His kingdom? One day Jesus spoke a parable about the importance of being ready for His return by watching and serving faithfully, and Peter asked, "Lord, are you telling this parable to us, or to everyone?" (Luke 12:41). Jesus replied by telling another parable about faithfulness, suggesting that both parables applied to all believers. The reality of the future kingdom isn't a topic for speculation; it's a motive for faithful, practical service today.

God's Word Can Be Trusted

One of the things Peter learned on the mount of transfiguration was the trustworthiness of God's prophetic Word. "And we have the word of the prophets made more certain," he wrote, "and you will do well to pay attention to it, as to a light shining in a dark place" (2 Peter 1:19). Spiritual experiences come and go, and the memories of these experiences may fade, but the Word of the Lord abides and never changes. What Peter, James, and John saw and heard on the mount corroborated the words of the prophets. Peter compared the prophetic Word to a "light shining in a dark place." The word translated *dark* means "murky," like a dark cellar or a dismal swamp. What an image for this present evil world! To the unsaved person, the world system is a garden, but to the person who has "tasted the goodness of the word of God and the powers of the coming age" (Heb. 6:5), this world is a dark, murky swamp!

When Jesus was on earth, the world rejected Him and shouted, "We have no king but Caesar" (John 19:15). Jesus wore a crown of thorns, and His kingship was mocked. Today, though, He reigns in heaven as God's anointed King-Priest, and one day He will return to judge the world and establish His kingdom. We don't know the day or the hour of His return, so we need to pay attention to the prophetic Word and do our work faithfully so we can stand before His presence unashamed.

Suffering Can Lead to Glory

Perhaps the most important lesson Peter learned was that suffering can lead to glory. It so impressed him that he devoted a good part of his first epistle to declaring it. Peter initially opposed Jesus dying on the cross because he saw no connection between suffering and glory. Even the Old Testament prophets who wrote the Word didn't fully understand "the sufferings of Christ and the glories that would follow" (1 Peter 1:10–12). In one prophecy, they saw a suffering Messiah, but in another, they beheld a glorious king. Were there two Messiahs, one who would suffer and one who would reign? Like the two discouraged disciples on the way to Emmaus, the Twelve needed to understand all that the prophets had spoken and realize that Messiah had to suffer shame and death before He could enter into His glory (Luke 24:25–27).

In his two epistles, Peter mentions *suffering* at least eighteen times and *glory* sixteen times—so he got the message! After all, if our Lord had to suffer before He could enter into His glory, why should His followers expect an easier way? As Paul and Barnabas taught young believers, "We must go through many hardships to enter the kingdom of God" (Acts 14:22). Jesus Himself told His followers, "Whoever serves me must follow me; and where I am, my servant also will be" (John 12:26). Peter said it like this:

Dear friends, do not be surprised at the painful trial you are suffering, as though something strange were happening to you. But rejoice that you participate in the sufferings of Christ, so that you may be overjoyed when his glory is revealed. If you are insulted because of the name of

Christ, you are blessed, for the Spirit of glory and of God rests on you.

1 Peter 4:12–14

Suffering doesn't automatically lead to glory, however, even in the life of the Christian believer. Unless we claim God's promises, live by faith, and depend on the Holy Spirit, our suffering could make us bitter instead of better. When it comes to suffering for Christ, we must accept it, rejoice in it, and depend on the Spirit to give us grace to glorify the Lord in all things. As Peter counseled, "Humble yourselves, therefore, under God's mighty hand, that he may lift you up in due time. Cast all your anxiety on him because he cares for you" (1 Peter 5:6–7).

Heaven is a place of glory and joy, and hell is a place of sorrow and suffering. Here on earth we have a mixture of suffering and glory, sorrow and joy. Our suffering for Christ, though, can lead to glory if we trust and obey. In the past, those who have gladly suffered for Christ have brought great glory to His name and great blessing to His church. When Satan offered Jesus all the kingdoms of this world as payment for worshiping him (Matt. 4:8–10), he was promising Him glory without suffering; but Jesus knew that Satan's offers always lead to suffering without glory!

For faithful Christians, there's no way to escape suffering, but there is a way to *enlist* suffering so that it works for us and not against us. How do we do this? By committing ourselves to God and trusting His love and will. Paul wrote to the church at Rome, "I consider that our present sufferings are not worth comparing with the glory that will be revealed in us" (Rom. 8:18). And to the Corinthians he said, "Therefore we do not lose heart. Though outwardly we are wearing away, yet inwardly we are being renewed day by day. For our light and momentary troubles are achieving for us an eternal glory that far outweighs them all" (2 Cor. 4:16–17).

We Can Experience the Glory Now

The word *transfigured* used in Matthew 17:2 and Mark 9:2 describes a change on the outside that is generated from the inside. The Greek word gives us our English word *metamorphosis*, the process in nature by which living creatures change from an immature stage into an adult stage. The tadpole becomes the frog and the caterpillar turns into a butterfly or moth. These are not surface changes caused by addition but radical changes from the inside caused by dynamic transformation.

Those who know Jesus as Savior and Lord already have God's glory within, for Jesus said, "I have given them the glory that you gave me" (John 17:22). He promises that we shall behold His glory when we get to heaven (John 17:24). *But we can experience His glory today and have a personal "transfiguration" that transforms our lives and makes us a blessing to others.* Two key Scripture passages apply the word *transfigured* to Christian believers:

> Therefore, I urge you, brothers, in view of God's mercy, to offer your bodies as living sacrifices, holy and pleasing to God—this is your spiritual act of worship. Do not conform any longer to the pattern of this world, but be transformed [transfigured] by the renewing of your mind. Then you will be able to test and approve what God's will is—his good, pleasing and perfect will.
>
> Romans 12:1–2

> And we, who with unveiled faces all reflect [contemplate] the Lord's glory, are being transformed [transfigured] into his likeness with ever-increasing glory, which comes from the Lord, who is the Spirit.
>
> 2 Corinthians 3:18

The first passage compares us to sacrifices on the altar, but we are *living* sacrifices and not dead ones, and we belong totally to the Lord. We refuse to conform to the cheap things of this world, seeking only to be conformed to Jesus Christ. Daily we give to the Lord our body, mind, and will, and we ask Him to renew our minds through His Word so that our lives will be transfigured and radiate His glory. We must surrender body, mind, and will to the Lord daily and say no to the pattern of this world.

A transfigured life requires a renewed mind, and the Holy Spirit accomplishes this renewing as we expose ourselves to the Word of God. That's where the second passage comes in. The Word is compared to a mirror, and as the believer looks into the mirror of the Word, he or she sees Jesus Christ in His glory. As we meditate on Christ and the truth in His Word, the Spirit of God transforms us—transfigures us—and we become more and more like the Lord Jesus Christ. This is a lifelong process, and it demands a lifelong discipline of taking time to be holy. As Peter counseled us:

> Therefore, prepare your minds for action; be self-controlled; set your hope fully on the grace to be given you when Jesus Christ is revealed. As obedient children, do not conform to the evil desires you had when you lived in ignorance. But just as he who called you is holy, so be holy in all you do; for it is written: "Be holy, because I am holy."
>
> 1 Peter 1:13–16

Peter calls this transforming process purifying "yourselves by obeying the truth" (v. 22).

The context of 2 Corinthians 3:18 is Exodus 34, when Moses came down from Mount Sinai and didn't know that his face was radiating God's glory (Exod. 34:29–35). But the glory would fade away, so he wore a veil before the people so they wouldn't see the glory disappear. When he returned to meet God, he took off the veil and regained the glory. Paul saw this as a contrast to the experience of Christians today. We have nothing to hide, so we need no veil; and the glory we radiate comes from within and is increasing, not decreasing. As we spend time in God's presence and focus on Christ in the Word, we become more like Jesus Christ and reveal His glory in daily life. We may not see this glory in ourselves, but others will see it and be helped by it.

"Grace is but glory begun," wrote Jonathan Edwards, "and glory is but grace perfected." The psalmist wrote, "The LORD will give grace and glory" (Ps. 84:11 KJV), and He will—if we take time to be holy.

A Christian's Death Means Freedom

On the mount of transfiguration, Moses and Elijah spoke with Jesus "about his departure, which he was about to bring to fulfillment at Jerusalem" (Luke 9:31). The word translated *departure* is *exodos* and gives us our English word "exodus." Peter used this word when speaking about his impending death: "And I will make every effort to see that after my departure [*exodos*] you will always be able to remember these things" (2 Peter 1:15).

Moses had led Israel's exodus from the bondage of Egypt, and Elijah had delivered the nation from their bondage to idolatry (1 Kings 18). But Jesus would accomplish redemption from sin for the whole world by His sacrificial death on the cross: "For he [God] has rescued us from the dominion of darkness and brought us into the kingdom of the Son he loves, in whom we have redemption, the forgiveness of sins" (Col. 1:13–14). When you trust Jesus Christ, you enter into freedom.

Peter knew that he would die in the service of Christ and the church and that his death would bring glory to God (John 21:18–19). Our Lord's description is that of a person being crucified, and tradition tells us that Peter asked to be crucified head downward because he felt he wasn't worthy to die exactly as his Master died. That Peter should use the word *exodos* as a synonym for the death of a believer gives us something to think about.

Unlike Jesus, Peter wouldn't be delivering anybody else through his death, but the Lord would be delivering him from "the tent of this body" (2 Peter 1:13). Peter would "put off" the tent and go to be with the Lord, an image that Paul also used in 2 Corinthians 5:1–10. The body we now live in is but a temporary tent, a tabernacle indwelt by the Spirit of God; but one day we shall have a glorious new body. When we make our exodus from this body and this world, we trust we will have "a rich welcome into the eternal kingdom of our Lord and Savior Jesus Christ" (2 Peter 1:11). The picture is that of a triumphant Olympic contestant returning to his hometown to be honored.

If the transfiguration teaches us anything about death, it's that the death of a true believer involves the purpose of God and the glory of God. When we meet the last enemy, there's nothing to fear, because Jesus has already met death and soundly defeated him. Jesus has "destroyed death and has brought life and immortality to light through the gospel" (2 Tim. 1:10). Certainly we weep when loved ones leave us, but our sorrow is not hopeless (1 Thess. 4:13–18). A believer's death is but an exodus, a liberation.

Thinking about this reminds me of what evangelist D. L. Moody said when he was dying. "Earth recedes, heaven opens before me. No, this is no dream," he said to his son Will. "It is beautiful. . . . If this is death, it is sweet. There is no valley here. God is calling me, and I must go."[1] Years before he had said,

Some day you will read in the papers that D. L. Moody, of East Northfield, is dead. Don't you believe a word of it! At that moment, I shall be more alive than I am now. I shall have gone up higher, that is all—out of this old clay tenement into a house that is immortal; a body that death cannot touch, that sin cannot taint, a body fashioned like unto his glorious body.[2]

Exodus!

Even though the transfiguration involved James and John as well as Peter, and it didn't involve anything that Peter did, I want to include this miraculous experience because of its importance to Peter and to believers today. The transfiguration was an important event in the life of Jesus and the three disciples, and it shouldn't be ignored.

six

Hook, Line, and Taxes

Matthew 17:24-27

After Jesus and his disciples arrived in Capernaum, the collectors of the two-drachma tax came to Peter and asked, "Doesn't your teacher pay the temple tax?"

"Yes, he does," he replied.

When Peter came into the house, Jesus was the first to speak. "What do you think, Simon?" he asked. "From whom do the kings of the earth collect duty and taxes—from their own sons or from others?"

"From others," Peter answered.

"Then the sons are exempt," Jesus said to him. "But so that we may not offend them, go to the lake and throw out your line. Take the first fish you catch; open its mouth and you will find a four-drachma coin. Take it and give it to them for my tax and yours."

*W*hen you follow Jesus Christ, you never know what will happen next, because the life of faith is filled with surprises and new challenges. Peter, James, and John had no sooner come down from the mount of transfiguration than they saw Jesus cast a vicious demon out of a child. This miracle was followed by the Master once again telling the disciples about His coming crucifixion, an announcement they had difficulty understanding and accepting. It was from these glorious heights of revelation and power, along with a fearful view of the future, that Peter quickly descended into the everyday world of paying taxes. Jesus knew what was coming, however, and was perfectly adequate to handle the matter.

The temple officers asked Peter for the tax that Moses had established when the tabernacle was being constructed (Exod. 30:11–16). Each Jewish man twenty years old or older had to give half a shekel, and the silver was used to cast the blocks on which the tabernacle frame stood (38:25–27). The tax was supposed to be received whenever there was a national census, but it became an annual event. The money was used for the upkeep of the tabernacle and later the temple, as well as for the special sacrifices and supplies that the priests needed for their daily ministry at the sanctuary. But even more, the tax was a reminder to the people that they had been redeemed by the Lord from the bondage of Egypt. The half-shekel tax was the equivalent of two days' wages and was to be paid at Passover. However, when the officers approached Peter, it was nearly time for the Feast of Tabernacles, so Jesus and Peter were several months delinquent in paying the tax!

While this miracle wasn't as glorious as Christ's transfiguration or as public and dramatic as His casting the demon out of the child, it nevertheless reveals in a unique way the character of Jesus Christ and His compassionate care for His own.

Deity—Jesus Is God

Between the time Peter said *yes* to the tax collectors and then entered the house, he was probably figuring out how to pay the taxes; but Jesus anticipated him and spoke first. Jesus knew what had transpired outside the house, not because He was eavesdropping but because He is God. As with the feeding of the five thousand, the Lord "already had in mind what he was going to do" (John 6:6). God not only knows future events but has already considered every possible exigency and decided what He will do, and what He decides is always the best. *Providence* means "to see beforehand," and the Lord is never surprised by any circumstance. He is Jehovah-Jireh—"the Lord who sees to it" (Gen. 22:14). St. Augustine wrote, "Trust the past to the mercy of God, the present to His love, and the future to His providence." Before we tell God what we think He should do, let's listen to what He wants to do. It will save us a great deal of time and trouble.

When you consider the complexity of this miracle of the coin and the fish, you can't help but acknowledge the deity of Jesus Christ. First, somebody had to drop a coin into the Sea of Galilee just as a fish was passing by. As every fisherman knows, fish will go after bright objects moving in the water, but this fish really had to hustle. If it waited too long, the coin would be lost in the debris on the bottom of the sea. The fish had to grasp the coin but not swallow it, and the coin had to lodge in the fish's mouth in such a way that the fish wouldn't be choked but would be able to take the bait on Peter's hook. Peter had to drop his baited hook where the fish would see it, and the fish had to go after the bait even though it had a coin lodged in its mouth. The fish also had to get to Peter's bait before any other fish got there!

The working of the providence of God is a mystery we can't explain, but it is also a marvel we can behold. The prophet Ezekiel saw the glorious throne of God moving about on wheels within wheels (Ezek. 1), a demonstration of the sovereign will of God at work in the world. The wheels of God's providence are always turning and changing directions, interfacing and intersecting, accomplishing His divine purposes in ways that we don't always see and can't begin to comprehend.

Before we leave this topic, we need to consider Peter's part in this miracle. Was he wrong in telling the tax collectors that Jesus paid the temple tax? Perhaps he should have consulted the Master first and then reported His answer. I may be wrong, but it seems to me that Peter was acting wisely by replying as he did, for it was possible that the officers were part of a scheme to trap Jesus. The tax was already six months overdue, and the officers may have delayed visiting Jesus just so they could accuse Him. In the Greek text, their question is phrased in such a way that they expected a negative answer: "Your teacher doesn't pay the temple tax, does he?" The Jewish Zealots, who violently opposed the Romans, refused to pay the tax because the temple was in the hands of pagans and functioned only by permission of Rome. Perhaps the tax officers wanted to identify Jesus with the rebels and give the chief priests and Pharisees ammunition to attack Him.

Also, Peter's willingness to use a hook and line is, to me, an indication of his growing humility and submission to Jesus. When he showed up at the Sea of Galilee, people must have smiled as they saw the well-known fisherman drop his baited hook into the water. Peter was now a follower of the Nazarene, and now this experienced fisherman had replaced his boats and nets with a line! Like a little boy, he was fishing for one fish when he might have used one of his boats and fished for scores of fish, sold them, and made some money. Little did the spectators realize that Peter was participating in a miracle that would be written in God's Word and for centuries read by people around the world.

Authority: Jesus Is King

This miracle is recorded only in the Gospel of Matthew, and Matthew's major theme is the kingdom of heaven. His book opens with, "A record of the genealogy of Jesus Christ the son of David, the son of Abraham" (Matt. 1:1). The title "Son of David" declares that Jesus is in the royal family and part of the Davidic dynasty. God had promised David that his dynasty would not end (2 Sam. 7:12–17), and this promise is fulfilled in Jesus Christ (Luke 1:30–33). Throughout his book, Matthew magnified our Lord's kingship and authority. Jesus taught as one having authority (Matt. 7:29), not like the scribes and Pharisees who only quoted "the authorities." He had the authority to heal (8:9), to forgive sin (9:6), and to conquer Satan (10:1). Matthew closed his book by quoting those magnificent words of Jesus, "All authority in heaven and on earth has been given to me" (28:18).

When God created the first man and woman, He gave them "rule over the fish of the sea and the birds of the air, over the livestock, over all the earth, and over all the creatures that move along the ground" (Gen. 1:26; see Ps. 8:5–8). King Adam and Queen Eve were coregents with the Lord as they tended the Garden and cared for its creatures. But when Adam and Eve sinned, they lost their crowns and scepters and forfeited their authority over creation. That's why Scripture says, "In putting everything under him [man], God left nothing that is not subject to him. Yet at present we do not see everything subject to him. But we see Jesus" (Heb. 2:8–9). Adam lost the dominion, but Jesus, the Last Adam, regained it!

Jesus demonstrated to Peter that He had dominion over the fish, for He enabled him to catch great numbers of fish in his nets as well as one specific fish on his hook. Peter would later learn that Jesus had dominion over the live-stock, for He would ride an unbroken donkey into Jerusalem (Mark 11:2–7). After he denied Christ three times, Peter heard the cock crow, and he learned the hard way that Jesus also had rule over the birds of the air (Mark 14:66–72). Yes, Jesus Christ has restored in Himself the dominion that Adam and Eve lost, and one day His people will share that reign with Him. In fact, as we yield to Him by faith, we today can "reign in life" through Jesus Christ (Rom. 5:17).

Humility: Jesus Is Servant

Jesus is God and King, and yet He didn't have even half a shekel in the treasury to pay the temple tax! "For you know the grace of our Lord Jesus Christ, that though he was rich, yet for your sakes he became poor, so that you through his poverty might become rich" (2 Cor. 8:9). In His reply to Peter, Jesus claimed to be the son of the King and therefore exempt from paying taxes, but He paid the tax just the same and proved His kingship in the way He did it.

Watchman Nee once wrote, "Any fool can be a king, but it takes a wise king to be a servant." Jesus willingly left heaven's throne and came to earth as a servant (Phil. 2:1–11). His obedience took Him to the cross, where as God's Suffering Servant He died for the sins of the world. "He himself bore our sins in his body on the tree" (1 Peter 2:24). As you read the Gospel records, you can't help but marvel at the display of authority and humility revealed in Jesus Christ. Every act of service was regal, and yet the King was the Servant!

Too many believers today have unconsciously adopted the world's idea of greatness—position, power, wealth, fame—and have forgotten that true greatness in God's kingdom means humility, sacrifice, and service. When His disciples argued over which of them was the greatest, Jesus simply said, "But I am among you as one who serves" (Luke 22:27). Behind many personal problems, family failures, and church conflicts you will often find dangerous people who want to be important and have their own way instead of being servants who seek God's way.

Jesus wasn't obligated to pay the temple tax. After all, He was the Redeemer and didn't need to pay "redemption money." He was the King and couldn't be taxed. Then why didn't He just forget the whole matter? Because there was a principle involved, and He explained it to Peter: "But so that we may not offend them" (Matt. 17:27). Jesus had every right to ignore paying the tax, but He willingly set aside His rights for the sake of others. It's a serious thing to cause others to stumble (see Matt. 18:1–10), but it's a blessed thing to set aside our own rights and privileges and "serve one another in love" (Gal. 5:13).

One of the major causes of division in the church today is the selfish way we insist that others agree with us. One of the greatest lessons I learned from the late Dr. Bob Cook was that God can bless people we disagree with—and He does! The early Christian assemblies in Rome were in danger of fragmenting because they didn't know how to exercise Christian love and build unity out of diversity. The more mature believers in the churches, who knew the meaning of Christian liberty, were offending the weaker Christians by their actions; and both groups were judging and criticizing each other and creating a climate of conflict in their meetings.

How did Paul seek to solve the problem? By pointing out that those who have been received by Christ had better receive one another (Rom. 14:1), and that it was the responsibility of the stronger saints to care for the weaker saints and give them the care they need to help them grow up (vv. 10–18). Isn't this what we do in our families? Don't parents and older children lovingly care for and protect the little ones and put up with their many mistakes so that the children can mature and one day enjoy life as responsible adults? That's what Paul called "serving one another in love."

But Jesus used another phrase that indicated His humility: "for my tax and yours" (Matt. 17:27). The original text reads simply, "for me and you." Jesus didn't say "for us," because though He was fully human, yet in His incarnation He was still the holy Son of God. That's why He told Mary Magdalene to tell the disciples, "I am returning to my Father and your Father, and to my God and your God" (John 20:17). Nevertheless, Jesus identified Himself with Peter and his need, just as He identifies Himself with us and our needs today. As our High Priest, Jesus sympathizes with our weaknesses (Heb. 4:14–16) and provides what we need (Phil. 4:19). But when we come to His throne of grace, let's be sure that what we ask is "for Him" as well as "for us," lest we be found asking selfishly just to please ourselves. That's one reason why "Hallowed be your name" is the first request in the Lord's Prayer (Matt. 6:9)—glorifying God is the fundamental motive for true prayer.

When Jesus paid the temple tax, He identified Himself with Peter and every other Jewish man who also paid it. But *the way He paid the tax* set Him apart from everybody else. In everything, Jesus still has the supremacy (Col. 1:18).

Credibility: Jesus Is Faithful

We've seen some unique features of this miracle: it's recorded only by Matthew, it's the only miracle using money, and it's the only miracle Jesus performed to meet His own need. But perhaps the most remarkable feature of this miracle is that the miracle itself is not recorded! We expect to read

> 28 And Peter obeyed the Lord and went to the sea with his hook and line, and he caught a fish that had a coin in its mouth. It was just enough money to pay the temple tax for Jesus and himself.

In spite of the fact that there is no verse 28 in the text, does anybody doubt that this miracle actually occurred? Of course not! Why? Because what Jesus says will happen always happens. His commandments are His enablements: "For no word from God shall be void of power" (Luke 1:37 ASV). If we have faith to believe that this "unreported" miracle actually happened, then why don't we believe everything else Jesus has commanded and promised?

When we believe God's promises and commandments and act on them, God releases His power and accomplishes His purposes. Jesus could have produced the coin out of thin air, but miracles aren't "magic." Even God uses means to get His will done on earth, and Peter's faith, plus his hook and line, were a part of that means. "According to your faith will it be done to you" (Matt. 9:29) because "he who promised is faithful" (Heb. 10:23).

We would see more of Christ's miracle power in our own lives if, like Peter, we didn't try to "second guess" the Master but simply trusted Him and did what He told us to do.

seven

God's Grace in the Garden

Matthew 26:47–54; Mark 14:43–49;
Luke 22:47–53; John 18:1–11

While he was still speaking a crowd came up, and the man who was called Judas, one of the Twelve, was leading them. He approached Jesus to kiss him, but Jesus asked him, "Judas, are you betraying the Son of Man with a kiss?"

When Jesus' followers saw what was going to happen, they said, "Lord, should we strike with our swords?" And one of them struck the servant of the high priest, cutting off his right ear.

But Jesus answered, "No more of this!" And he touched the man's ear and healed him.

Then Jesus said to the chief priests, the officers of the temple guard, and the elders, who had come for him, "Am I leading a rebellion, that you have come with swords and clubs? Every day I was with you in the temple courts, and you did not lay a hand on me. But this is your hour—when darkness reigns."

Luke 22:47–53

*W*hen I meditate on our Lord's arrest in the Garden of Gethsemane, I get a mental picture of a cup, a kiss, and a sword. The cup represented the Father's will for His beloved Son, and Jesus took that cup and drank it to the full. The kiss displayed the treachery of Judas, and the sword demonstrated the bravery of Peter, sincere but misguided. All of us are imitating one of these three. Some are like the Savior, accepting God's will and obeying it; while some are like Judas, pretending to do God's will but betraying the Master. Perhaps too many of us are like Peter, resisting God's will and thinking we're doing the Lord a service by starting a fight. We need to consider Peter's sword and Malchus's ear, because this was the last miracle Jesus performed before He was arrested, tried, and crucified.

When you compare the accounts in the four Gospels, you discover some interesting facts. Only John gives us the name of the victim—Malchus—but John was "known to the high priest" (John 18:15), and Malchus was one of the servants of Caiaphas. Only John names Peter as the assailant (vv. 10–11), and only Luke tells us about the miracle of healing, but Luke was a physician (Luke 22:51). For the final miracle of His earthly ministry, this was certainly a modest demonstration of power, and probably few people noticed it. But then His first miracle was known only to His disciples and a few servants (John 2:8–9, 11), and Jesus never was one to magnify His miracles. However unassuming this miracle might be, everything about it glorifies the grace of God.

God's Grace to Malchus

The armed mob that came into the Garden to arrest Jesus included a large number of Roman soldiers as well as members of the temple guard and individuals from "the establishment" who wanted to be in on the action. Among them was Malchus, servant to Caiaphas, the high priest, who may have been there by order of his master. Jerusalem was crowded with passionately patriotic Jews, so the high priest had no trouble securing Roman soldiers to handle the arrest. Rome certainly didn't want any riots during Passover. It's likely that Malchus knew Judas and walked with him as he led the soldiers to Jesus. Caiaphas was determined to have Jesus killed (John 11:47–53), and it appears that Malchus heartily agreed with his master. Being at the front of that arresting mob wasn't the safest place in Jerusalem that night, but Malchus was determined to see his master's orders obeyed. How tragic that a religious leader, and a high priest at that, would turn his servant into an enemy of the Son of God.

Did Peter strike out with his sword because Malchus actually laid hands on Jesus? Or was Peter aiming for Judas and accidentally hit Malchus? Did Peter even know who Malchus was? These questions aren't answered in the biblical text, and it's unprofitable for us to speculate. It all happened so quickly that most of the people in the Garden didn't even know a miracle had occurred. But the fact that a miracle did occur is evidence of the grace of the Lord. Would you have healed a common slave who was part of a conspiracy to crucify you? Jesus did—and that's grace.

Theologians tell us that grace means God gives us what we don't deserve, and mercy means He doesn't give us what we do deserve. In the days of David the king, a man named Uzzah touched the ark of God and God killed him (2 Sam. 6:1–10); yet Malchus helped to arrest the Son of God and the Lord healed him! James and John once suggested that Jesus incinerate the stubborn inhabitants of a Samaritan village, but Jesus rebuked them and reminded them that He came to save people's lives and not destroy them (Luke 9:51–56; see also John 3:17). Malchus and the soldiers were included when Jesus prayed from the cross, "Father, forgive them, for they do not know what they are doing" (Luke 23:34).

Jesus taught His disciples to return love for hatred (Matt. 5:43–45), and He practiced what He preached. Peter wrote about it in his first epistle:

> Christ suffered for you, leaving you an example, that you should follow in his steps.
> "He committed no sin,
>   and no deceit was found in his mouth."
> When they hurled their insults at him, he did not retaliate; when he suffered, he made no threats.
>
> 1 Peter 2:21–23

The Father could have sent twelve legions of angels (that's 72,000 angels) to rescue His Son, a legion for each of the eleven disciples and one for Jesus, but this wasn't the Father's plan. The mob didn't realize it, but in the suffering and death of Jesus, God was demonstrating His love and grace (Rom. 5:8).

Did Malchus ever believe on Jesus and become a Christian? We hope so, but we don't know for sure. But he experienced a miracle! Yes, but miracles don't automatically generate saving faith in the hearts of sinners. When Jesus raised Lazarus from the dead, some of the witnesses believed on Him and were saved, but others went and told His enemies what had happened (John 11:45–46). "Even after

Jesus had done all these miraculous signs in their presence, they still would not believe in him" (John 12:37).

This we know: Jesus revealed His grace to Malchus by stopping Peter from continuing his attack and then by healing his ear. Malchus had more evidence for believing on Christ than did the thief on the cross, and we hope he made good use of his opportunity.

God's Grace to Peter

One of the favorite occupations of too many teachers and preachers is "bashing" the people whose Bible biographies record their blunders and sins, especially Jacob and Peter, and yet none of us is worthy to carry their sandals let alone report their sins. A. W. Tozer's assessment is correct: "Anyway, we are glad Peter lived, and we are glad Christ found him. He is so much like so many of us, at least in his weaknesses. It only remains for us to learn also the secret of his strength."[1] And while we're learning, let's keep in mind the admonition of Paul, "So, if you think you are standing firm, be careful that you don't fall!" (1 Cor. 10:12). We're all made of clay, and we haven't yet become rocks!

From sharing the Seder in the upper room to wielding the sword in the Garden, Peter had walked a difficult and dangerous path, and he would confess that the difficulties and dangers were of his own making. He spoke when he should have been listening, boasted when he should have been fearing, slept when he should have been praying, and fought when he should have been submitting. Simon Peter attacked the wrong enemy, for it was Satan and not Malchus who was in control that night (Luke 22:53). Peter displayed the wrong attitude and once again tried to keep Jesus from going to the cross (Matt. 16:21–23; 17:4). He used the wrong energy and the wrong weapon, for we can't battle the forces of hell in our own strength and without the sword of the Spirit (Eph. 6:10–18). Jesus had warned Peter, but Peter's spiritual hearing was impaired.

While we don't excuse Peter, nor do we want to imitate him, in all fairness we have to consider two factors. The first factor involves what Peter said. After the Lord warned him and the other disciples that they would fail Him, Peter boasted of his love for Christ and his willingness to go to prison and death for Him (Luke 22:31–34; John 13:37). When you make a claim like that, you try to live up to it. While we may admire Peter's zeal and courage, we're pained when we think of his ignorance and impulsiveness. Even more, we're pained when we think of our own foolish actions and words that have cut others.

The second factor is that Jesus had actually spoken to His disciples about swords.

> Then Jesus asked them, "When I sent you without purse, bag or sandals, did you lack anything?" "Nothing," they answered. He said to them, "But now if you have a purse, take it, and also a bag; and if you don't have a sword, sell your cloak and buy one. It is written, 'And he was numbered with the transgressors'; and I tell you that this must be fulfilled in me. Yes, what is written about me is reaching its fulfillment." The disciples said, "See, Lord, here are two swords." "That is enough," he replied.
>
> Luke 22:35–38

It's clear that the disciples failed to understand Jesus' message, because they took His words literally. When the disciples had gone out on their mission (Matt. 10), Jesus was still recognized as a great teacher and large crowds followed Him. But now He would be treated like a transgressor *and the disciples' situation would change radically.* They would face opposition from the enemy, and they needed to expect it and prepare for it. Our Lord's words, "That is enough," were spoken in sadness and indicated that He was grieved at their lack of insight. You don't defend or extend Christ's spiritual kingdom by using physical weapons (John 18:36–37) but by using the sword of the Spirit, as Peter did at Pentecost (Acts 2; compare Heb. 4:12).

Peter misunderstood and misapplied the Word of God and therefore disobeyed the Lord; but Jesus in His grace rescued him. He stopped Peter from making further use of the sword, and He repaired the damage Peter had done to Malchus. Had the Savior not intervened, the Roman soldiers might have taken Peter into custody along with Jesus. When he dictated his first epistle to Silas, I wonder if this event in the Garden came to Peter's mind when he said: "Submit yourselves for the Lord's sake to every authority instituted among men" (1 Peter 2:13), or, "Do not repay evil with evil or insult with insult, but with blessing" (3:9), or, "If you suffer, it should not be as a murderer or thief" (4:15). Do Peter's words come to our minds when we're tempted to fight back? I may be wrong, but I have a feeling that more harm has been done to the work of Christ on earth by zealous disciples like Peter wielding their swords than by hypocrites like Judas giving their kisses.

Most people don't carry swords these days, but we often damage others by what we impulsively say and do. "Reckless words pierce like a sword, but the tongue of the wise brings healing" (Prov. 12:18). Perhaps if we had the cup in our hands, we wouldn't be using the sword.

God's Grace to a Sinful World

You and I weren't in the Garden with Jesus when Peter became a one-man army to defend Him, but we have certainly benefited from what happened there that night. Had Jesus taken the sword instead of the cup, He would not have died on the cross, and we would still be in our sins.

"Put your sword away!" Jesus said to Peter. "Shall I not drink the cup the Father has given me?" (John 18:11).

Among other things, drinking from a cup is a biblical image for surrendering to the will of God and experiencing the suffering that it brings. Jesus gave up His reputation and was classified with the criminals. He gave up His civil rights and was treated like a dangerous animal instead of like a harmless man. The trial was rigged, the governor was intimidated, and the prisoner was tortured—but the religious leaders felt good because they were "doing the will of God." Jesus could have summoned 72,000 angels to deliver Him, but He took the cup and drank it to the dregs. In King Hezekiah's day, one angel killed 185,000 enemy soldiers (Isa. 37:36), so twelve legions of angels could have wiped out more than 13 billion people!

He could have saved Himself, but He chose to save us. "And we have seen and testify," wrote the apostle John, "that the Father has sent his Son to be the Savior of the world" (1 John 4:14). God's grace was present in the Garden and at the cross at Calvary. God's grace is available to us from the throne of grace where Jesus reigns in glory. "From the fullness of his grace we have all received one blessing after another" (John 1:16). Peter wrote that He is "the God of all grace" (1 Peter 5:10). And who knew better than Peter?

eight

A Little Bird Told Him

Matthew 26:57-75; Mark 14:53-72;
Luke 22:54-62; John 18:15-27

Then seizing him, they led him away and took him into
the house of the high priest. Peter followed at a distance.
But when they had kindled a fire in the middle of the courtyard and had sat down together, Peter sat down with them.
A servant girl saw him seated there in the firelight. She
looked closely at him and said, "This man was with him."

But he denied it. "Woman, I don't know him," he said.

A little later someone else saw him and said, "You also
are one of them."

"Man, I am not!" Peter replied.

About an hour later another asserted, "Certainly this
fellow was with him, for he is a Galilean."

Peter replied, "Man, I don't know what you're talking about!" Just as he was speaking, the rooster crowed. The Lord turned and looked straight at Peter. Then Peter remembered the word the Lord had spoken to him: "Before the rooster crows today, you will disown me three times." And he went outside and wept bitterly.

Luke 22:54–62

*A*nd Peter followed afar off" is a favorite text of preachers. The statement is found in all the Gospels except John, so it can't be ignored (Matt. 26:58; Mark 14:54; Luke 22:54)—but it can be misinterpreted, and often it is. On checking the index of the published sermons in my library, I was surprised to discover that four famous preachers all took this text and preached about "the distant disciple" and the danger of "following Christ at a distance." Their sermons were excellent but had no connection with the text because they completely missed the point.

When you read the Gospel accounts carefully, you discover that Peter and the other disciples *weren't supposed to follow Jesus at all.* Jesus wanted them to get out of the Garden as soon as possible. When they left the upper room, Jesus reminded them of Zechariah 13:7: "Strike the shepherd, and the sheep will be scattered" (see also Matt. 26:31; Mark 14:27)—a clear announcement that He wanted the men to leave. Furthermore, when the mob arrived and Jesus boldly confronted them, He said, "If you are looking for me, then let these men go" (John 18:8). This was our Lord's way of dismissing His disciples from the Garden. He had promised to meet them after His resurrection, and that promise was all they needed to sustain them during the few difficult days that lay before them. But the signal was clear: Get away!

The disciples did flee the scene, but disobeying his Master's orders, Peter followed the mob and ended up in the high priest's courtyard, where he denied his Lord three times. Peter wasn't the "blessed man" of Psalm 1:1, because he walked in the counsel of the ungodly instead of in the counsel of the Lord; then he stood with sinners (John 18:18), and finally he sat with the scornful by the fire (Luke 22:55). The same night that Jesus sweat great drops of blood, Peter was cold and had to sit by the enemy's fire.

Mark tells us that the rooster crowed twice (Mark 14:72), so the first crowing was an advance warning that Peter ignored. After Peter had denied the Lord the third time, the rooster crowed again. At that moment, Luke reports, the Lord turned and looked at Peter (Luke 22:61), and Luke used the same word John used when he described our Lord's first meeting with Peter (John 1:42). It was a tender, penetrating look of love and understanding, not a scowl of condemnation. This time the message of the bird reached Peter's heart and he began to weep, and he left the courtyard and went out and wept bitterly.

Self-righteous people who rejoice that they're not like other men criticize Peter severely for what he did, but Christians who know their own hearts and have also heard the crowing of the cock sympathize with the fisherman. They don't approve of his sin, of course; but they do identify with his pain, for they too have wept in secret and wished to turn back the clock and do things differently. It is to Peter's credit that he was brought to repentance by such a natural and simple thing, an event that occurred every morning—the crowing of a rooster. Invisible sound waves from the mouth of a bird reached the man's heart and brought him to his senses. It took a famine and a prison experience to make Joseph's brothers finally tell the truth, and Jonah had to go through a storm and a near-death experience before he came to his senses. But all it took to break Peter's heart was the crowing of a rooster and a look from Jesus.

The crowing of the cock conveyed three messages to Peter, and these messages are still valid for us to hear today whenever we fail the Lord.

Reassurance: Jesus Christ Is Lord!

No matter how discouraging the circumstances around us or how painful the feelings within us, Jesus Christ is still Lord. He was arrested and bound, but He was Lord. Evil men pushed Him from one trial to another, but He was Lord. He was humiliated and mocked, but He was Lord. He was physically weak, but He was Lord. One of His own disciples had betrayed Him, but He was Lord. Peter would deny Him three times, but He was Lord. Peter's world had fallen apart, but Jesus Christ was still Lord of all. He didn't demonstrate His lordship by doing a remarkable public miracle. All He did was keep every bird in Jerusalem quiet and then at the right time command one rooster to crow.

When we meditated on the miracle of the tax money, we learned that Jesus Christ is the Second Adam who has regained the dominion that the first Adam lost when he sinned. Peter had seen Jesus exercise dominion over the fish (Luke 5) and over the beasts (Mark 11:1–7), but now he experienced His dominion over the birds. Certainly it's a natural thing for a rooster to crow in the morning, but Jesus made sure he crowed at the right time and that no other birds joined him.

"But this is your hour—when darkness reigns," Jesus told the mob (Luke 22:53), but in saying this He was neither abdicating the throne nor excusing their conduct ("The devil made us do it"). God's Suffering Servant was submitted to God's sovereign will, and this was the hour He had spoken about from the beginning of His ministry and prayed about as He faced its fulfillment (John 2:4; 17:1). It looked like Satan was having his way, but it was the Lord who was in control. In those hours when darkness seems to reign, it's good to know that God is still on the throne.

Repentance: You Can Be Forgiven!

During their time in the upper room, Peter had heard Jesus say many important things. We don't know how much of the Word really lodged in his mind and heart, but surely he recalled, "Simon, Simon, Satan has asked to sift you [all the disciples] as wheat. But I have prayed for you, Simon, that your faith may not fail. And when you have turned back, strengthen your brothers" (Luke 22:31–32). The power of darkness could do nothing without the permission of the God of light, and none of Satan's devices could succeed against the prayers of the Savior. Three times Jesus called Peter "Simon," which was his old name, as if to warn him that the old man he used to be was about to take over. Peter's courage did fail, but his faith didn't and he was forgiven and restored. Jesus didn't say, "If you are turned back," but, "When you are turned back."

Peter wasn't the first person in Bible history to fail in his strongest point, which in his case was his courage. Abraham's greatest strength was his faith, but it was his faith that failed when twice he ran off and lied about his wife (Gen. 12:10–20; 20:1–18) and also when he "married" Hagar in order to have a son (Gen. 16). Moses was a man of great humility (Num. 12:3), but he lost his temper and hit the rock and forfeited entering the Promised Land (Num. 20). David's greatest strength was his integrity, but that's where he failed when he attempted to cover up his sins of adultery and murder (2 Sam. 11–12). In our weakest points, we often tempt ourselves, but Satan knows how to attack our strongest points.

Matthew, Mark, and Luke all inform us that when the rooster crowed, "Peter remembered the word" and went out and wept bitterly (Matt. 26:75; Mark 14:72; Luke 22:61–62). During that evening, Peter had resisted the Word, almost argued with Jesus, and then had disobeyed the Word and gone to sleep. He ran ahead of the Word when he drew his sword and attacked Malchus. But now he remembered the Word and left the place of danger and defeat for a place of repentance and restoration. "The sacrifices of God are a broken spirit; a broken and contrite heart, O God, you will not despise" (Ps. 51:17).

True repentance is much more than regret or remorse. Judas regretted what he did to Jesus, but his remorse drove him to suicide. Peter's repentance led him to confession and cleansing, and the Lord met with him privately to assure him of forgiveness (1 Cor. 15:3–5). "But go, tell his disciples and Peter, 'He is going ahead of you into Galilee'" (Mark 16:7), the angel told the women at the empty tomb. Those two words "and Peter" must have given Peter new courage and hope. The angel didn't include Peter among the disciples because Peter had betrayed them as well as the Master (Mark 14:69–71). Peter would make that right after breakfast one morning and would hear Jesus say to him once again, "Follow me!" (John 21:15–19).

When Satan tempts us to sin, he often whispers to us, "You can get away with this." But after we've disobeyed the Lord, Satan repeatedly shouts at us, "You'll never get away with it!" and tries to convince us that all hope is gone. Sometimes the despair of a disobedient saint is worse than the conviction of a lost sinner. Instead of listening to the accusations of Satan, we must tune our ear to the invitations of our Lord and, like Peter, remember the Word.

> Seek the LORD while he may be found;
>   call on him while he is near.
> Let the wicked forsake his way

and the evil man his thoughts.
Let him turn to the LORD, and he will have mercy on him,
and to our God, for he will freely pardon.

Isaiah 55:6–7

But with you there is forgiveness;
therefore you are feared.

Psalm 130:4

"I, even I, am he who blots out
your transgressions, for my own sake,
and remembers your sins no more."

Isaiah 43:25

Who is a God like you,
who pardons sin and forgives the transgression
of the remnant of his inheritance?
You do not stay angry forever
but delight to show mercy.

Micah 7:18

If we confess our sins, he is faithful and just and will forgive us our sins and purify us from all unrighteousness.

1 John 1:9

Renaissance: It's the Dawning of a New Day!

That is the message the rooster announces every morning: "Wake up! Get going! It's a new day! No matter what happened yesterday, you can begin anew." George Morrison used to say that the victorious Christian life is a series of new beginnings, and he was right. Peter had sinned, but the sun still came up and was a reminder that God had not forsaken

His covenant with Israel or with David that David's son would reign forever (Jer. 33:19–22; 2 Sam. 7). The Son of David wasn't being treated too royally by Caesar's soldiers, but just wait until the first day of the week!

Satan may have been free to work during an hour of darkness, but Jesus was ushering in a day of light and grace. As the psalmist promised, "Weeping may remain for a night, but rejoicing comes in the morning" (Ps. 30:5). And as Jeremiah wrote, "Because of the LORD'S great love we are not consumed, for his compassions never fail. They are new every morning; great is your faithfulness" (Lam. 3:22–23). That bird had something to crow about when he announced the dawning of a new day!

The life of Christian discipleship isn't like a missile that's shot into the air and never deviates from its course. Following Jesus is more like walking through "a land of mountains and valleys" (Deut. 11:11), where sometimes we stumble or wander off on detours. But our cries of confession bring Jesus to our side, and He takes us back to the main road and gives us a fresh beginning.

After sinning in Egypt, Abraham returned to the place where he had disobeyed God, and he started over again (Gen. 13:1–4). After years of trial and testing, Jacob returned to Bethel, the place where he had first met the Lord (Gen. 35), and God began to write a glorious new chapter in his biography. King David paid dearly because he sinned, for, as Charles Spurgeon said, "An ordinary sinner sins cheaply, but the child of God sins very dearly." But God heard David's confession and forgave his sins and gave him a new beginning. He heard the crowing of the cock, as we all must when the Lord convicts us, but he also saw the rising of the sun because God had cleansed and comforted him.

Jesus met Peter privately on the first day of the week and forgave him; later He met him again and restored him to his discipleship (John 21). The Lord frequently met with the eleven disciples during the forty days before His ascension to the Father, and ten days later He sent the Spirit to empower the infant church to be His witnesses. The crowing of the cock and the coming of the Spirit made Peter into a new man. He preached with power at Pentecost, and three thousand people repented and trusted Christ (Acts 2). He preached a second sermon, and two thousand more turned to the Savior (Acts 3–4). There are seven speeches from Peter recorded in the Book of Acts, which isn't too bad for a man whose speech occasionally got him into trouble.

No matter how far true disciples may stray from the Lord, they can always make a new beginning. It was the dawning of a new day for Peter, but not for Judas. "As soon as Judas had taken the bread, he went out. And it was night" (John 13:30). Alas, for Judas, it is still night, and it always will be night.

nine

THANKS FOR THE MEMORY

John 21:1–14

Afterward Jesus appeared again to his disciples, by the Sea of Tiberias. It happened this way: Simon Peter, Thomas (called Didymus), Nathanael from Cana in Galilee, the sons of Zebedee, and two other disciples were together. "I'm going out to fish," Simon Peter told them, and they said, "We'll go with you." So they went out and got into the boat, but that night they caught nothing.

Early in the morning, Jesus stood on the shore, but the disciples did not realize that it was Jesus.

He called out to them, "Friends, haven't you any fish?"

"No," they answered.

He said, "Throw your net on the right side of the boat and you will find some." When they did, they were unable to haul the net in because of the large number of fish.

Then the disciple whom Jesus loved said to Peter, "It is the Lord!" As soon as Simon Peter heard him say, "It is the Lord," he wrapped his outer garment around him (for he had taken it off) and jumped into the water. The other disciples followed in the boat, towing the net full of fish, for they were not far from shore, about a hundred yards. When they landed, they saw a fire of burning coals there with fish on it, and some bread.

Jesus said to them, "Bring some of the fish you have just caught."

Simon Peter climbed aboard and dragged the net ashore. It was full of large fish, 153, but even with so many the net was not torn. Jesus said to them, "Come and have breakfast." None of the disciples dared ask him, "Who are you?" They knew it was the Lord. Jesus came, took the bread and gave it to them, and did the same with the fish. This was now the third time Jesus appeared to his disciples after he was raised from the dead.

*I*t isn't so astonishing the number of things that I can remember, as the number of things I can remember that aren't so." The American humorist Josh Billings made that statement, and I can sympathize with him. When I wrote my autobiography a few years ago, I asked my two brothers and my sister to read the manuscript before I sent it to the publisher, and to my embarrassment they pointed out some serious errors. I was sure that I had recorded history, but in some cases it turned out to be fantasy. No wonder Oscar Wilde defined memory as "the diary that chronicles things that never have happened and couldn't possibly have happened."

Peter wrote his second epistle primarily to stir up his readers' memories so they wouldn't forget what he and the other apostles had taught them (2 Peter 1:12–15). "I think it is right to refresh your memory," he wrote, "and I will make every effort to see that after my departure you will always be able to remember these things." Peter no doubt recalled how his own memory had started him back on the road to recovery after he had denied the Lord. "Immediately a rooster crowed. Then Peter remembered the word Jesus had spoken: 'Before the rooster crows, you will disown me three times.' And he went outside and wept bitterly" (Matt. 26:74–75). Memory and conscience often work together.

But the experience that quickened Peter's memory the most is probably the one John recorded as a sort of appendix to his Gospel (John 21). Peter is mentioned at least thirteen times in this chapter, so the focus is on him and his Lord. There were at least two reasons why John wrote this appendix: (1) to explain how Peter was restored to fellowship and discipleship, and (2) to squelch the rumor that John would live until Jesus returned (John 21:20–24). It's remarkable how God's people can twist the words of Jesus and make them say what they were never meant to say.

Let's consider Peter's meeting with the resurrected Christ, the miracles that occurred, and how all of this helped Peter remember his past and prepare for his future.

He Remembered His Call to Discipleship (John 21:1–11)

In the upper room, Jesus promised to meet the disciples in Galilee after He arose from the dead (Matt. 26:31). On that resurrection day, both Jesus and the angel at the tomb repeated this message (Matt. 28:7, 10), and the angel even gave a special word for Peter (Mark 16:7). So the men went to Galilee and waited for Jesus to arrive.

Sometimes waiting is more difficult than working, especially if you're an impulsive fellow like Peter. One evening when seven of the disciples were together, Peter announced that he was going fishing, and the other six agreed to go with him. In doing this, I don't think they were announcing a return to the old life. It's just that Peter didn't enjoy just sitting around waiting and wanted to make good use of his time. If Jesus wanted to find them, He would know where they were.

When morning dawned, Peter found himself watching a rerun of what Luke recorded for us in the fifth chapter of his Gospel. In both scenarios, the men had fished all night and caught nothing, but when they followed the Lord's instructions, they had a great catch of fish. In the earlier experience, Peter was so overwhelmed that he fell at Jesus' knees and confessed his sinfulness. It was then that Jesus called Peter, Andrew, James, and John to become "fishers of men," and they left everything to follow Him. Since that event, Peter had denied both his calling and the Lord who had called him, so the experience John described in this chapter helped prepare him for his restoration.

As he sat on the shore that morning, surely Peter noticed not only the similarities in the two events but also the differences. In the earlier miracle, the nets began to break; this time, the net didn't break. The first time, they didn't know how many fish they had caught, and some of them had gotten away; but they had an exact count of the second catch—153 large fish, and none of them got away. In the first miracle, Peter had to call for help in handling the nets; now he was able to pull the net to shore by himself. But the same lesson from Jesus echoed in Peter's mind as he thought about both miracles: "Apart from me you can do nothing" (John 15:5).

John 21 records a really remarkable series of miracles. All night the men were prevented from catching any fish, and then they caught 153 large fish just by switching to the other side of the boat. (As George Morrison reminded us, the difference between success and failure was simply the width of the ship.) Six disciples together towed the net toward shore and then Peter had the strength to finish the job by himself. The net was full of large fish but it didn't break. On shore the disciples found a fire of coals with a meal already on it. It was quite an exciting way to start the day!

Once again Peter experienced the grace of the Lord Jesus Christ, for Jesus didn't lay down any conditions for blessing. He didn't promise him a miracle if he would first confess his sins. Jesus simply met the need and then healed the wounds. The Lord knew that Peter was thinking about the two miracles of the fish and recalling that he had left all to follow Jesus. Peter wanted to go on following Jesus, and that's exactly what Jesus invited him to do.

He Remembered His Confession of Christ (John 21:9, 12–14)

Seeing the bread and fish, Peter may have recalled the day when Jesus blessed the little boy's lunch and with it fed more than five thousand people (John 6:1–13). The miracle is described in all four Gospels, but only John gives us the sequel. The next day Jesus met part of that crowd in the Capernaum synagogue and gave them a sermon on the Bread of Life (John 6:25–59). The people knew about the manna that God sent from heaven to feed the Israelites in the wilderness, but they didn't realize that the very Bread of Life was right there in their presence.

Our Lord's sermon presented a series of contrasts. Through Moses, God gave Israel the manna, but the Father sent His Son to be the Bread of Life. The manna only sustained physical life, but Jesus *gives* eternal life. The manna was given only to Israel, but Jesus was sent to give life to the world. It did no good only to acknowledge the manna or look at it—you had to receive it and eat it. So with Jesus, the Bread of Life: You must receive Him by faith into your very being or He cannot save you. When the crowd heard

Jesus compare saving faith to eating His flesh and drinking His blood, they misunderstood His words and left Him. They knew it was against the law of Moses for a Jew to partake of human flesh or any kind of blood, and their spiritual blindness cost them salvation.

It was then that Jesus turned to the Twelve and asked, "You do not want to leave too, do you?" and Peter replied, "Lord, to whom shall we go? You have the words of eternal life. We believe and know that you are the Holy One of God" (John 6:67–69). Peter had made a similar confession at Caesarea Philippi: "You are the Christ, the Son of the living God" (Matt. 16:16).

But the memory of Peter's two confessions only made the fact of his three denials that much more painful. But those two confessions had been authentic, and Peter's fall had not destroyed his faith. He still belonged to Jesus, and Jesus belonged to him.

He Remembered His Denial of Christ (John 21:9)

"When they landed, they saw a fire of burning coals there" (John 21:9). The only other place you find the phrase "a fire of coals" in John's Gospel is in 18:18: "And the servants and officers who had made a fire of coals stood there. . . . And Peter stood with them" (NKJV). If anything on the shore that morning reminded Peter of what he had done, it was that fire of coals. Peter couldn't return to the place of his failure and make things right, but he could confess his sins to the One against whom he had sinned, and Jesus would forgive him and restore him.

From Peter's point of view, what sort of a place was that charcoal fire in the high priest's courtyard? For one thing, it was a source of heat, and Peter was cold. Peter was seeking comfort at a time when his Master was suffering humiliation and pain. It also seemed like a place of safety. He was sitting among the servants and the officers, and nobody would recognize him there. Two servant girls questioned Peter, but he managed to silence them. The third person who questioned him was a relative of Malchus, the man whose ear Peter had cut off (John 18:26–27). He too had been in the Garden when Jesus was arrested and was probably with Malchus and saw what happened. In the strongest language he knew, Peter denied the accusation, and then Jesus looked at him and the rooster crowed, and the masquerade was over.

Charles Spurgeon said that God doesn't allow His children to sin successfully, and Peter certainly proves him right. In spite of his attempts to remain anonymous, Peter gave himself away every time he said something (Matt. 26:73; Mark 14:70). Far from being a safe place, the enemy's fire was a most dangerous place for Peter to try to hide. The only safe place is in the will of God, and Peter wasn't there.

The scene by the fire on the shore of the Sea of Galilee, though, was a different experience, for there Peter was with his brothers in ministry. Take a coal out of that fire, and in a short time it's cold and needs to be rekindled. When Peter got away from the other disciples, he was an isolated coal, he grew cold and he sought a fire. But even more, there at the fire on the shore, Peter was with his Lord. There's no question that Peter dearly loved Jesus and that his failure wasn't because he had no love or faith. Even though Jesus had warned him of Satan's attack, Peter didn't watch and pray, and he walked right into the trap. No wonder Peter wrote, "Be self-controlled and alert. Your enemy the devil prowls around like a roaring lion looking for someone to devour" (1 Peter 5:8). Peter wasn't devoured, because the rooster defeated the lion—he had been very close to danger, and the Lord rescued him just in the nick of time.

He Remembered His Boast of Love (John 21:15–17)

"Even if all fall away on account of you, I never will," Peter had boasted. "Even if I have to die with you, I will never disown you" (Matt. 26:33, 35). Peter wasn't the only one who boasted that night; "all the other disciples said the same." Therefore, when Jesus began to probe Peter's heart, all of the men must have felt guilty. "Simon son of John, do you truly love me more than these?" (John 21:15). The phrase "more than these" probably refers to "these other disciples," because that's the way Peter stated his boast. "Even if all fall away on account of you, I never will." The fisherman had the same outlook as the proud man in the parable who prayed, "God, I thank you that I am not like other men" (Luke 18:11).

Three times Peter had publicly denied his Lord, and three times his Lord asked him if he truly loved Him.[1] After all, the most important requirement for servants of God is that they love their Lord, because if we love Him, we will obey Him. We hear a great deal about loving the saints, loving our enemies, loving lost souls, and loving our neighbors, but all of these flow out of our love for Jesus Christ. Shepherds with an ever-deepening love for Christ will love their people and speak God's truth in love. They will be peacemakers and not troublemakers, but they won't compromise the truth just to keep peace in the family. In 1757 John Newton wrote a letter to George Whitefield and among other things said:

> The longer I live, the more I see of the vanity and the sinfulness of our unchristian disputes; they eat up the very vitals of religion. . . . I allow that every branch of gospel truth is precious, that errors are abounding, and that it is our duty to bear an honest testimony to what the Lord has enabled us to find comfort in, and to instruct with meekness such as are willing to be instructed; but I cannot see it my duty, nay, I believe it would be my sin, to attempt to beat my notions into other people's heads. . . . When our dear Lord questioned Peter, after his fall and recovery, he said not, Art thou wise, learned and eloquent? nay, he said not, Art thou clear and sound, and orthodox? But this only,

"Lovest thou me?" An answer to this was sufficient then; why not now?[2]

Remember this admonition the next time you join in singing Newton's great song "Amazing Grace."

We show our love for Christ by loving His people, the little lambs as well as the maturing sheep. We feed the lambs and the sheep, and we shepherd the sheep, in the name of the Lord and because we love the Lord. Each believer has a spiritual gift to use to help the whole flock and the whole body, and if we love the Good Shepherd who died for us and the Great Shepherd who cares for us, we will love His people and minister to them. We will also allow them to minister to us. People who do this don't have to announce how much they love Christ because their works will say it for them.

Jesus gave the fisherman a new calling; now he would also serve as a shepherd. Jesus wasn't mixing metaphors or ministries. He was showing Peter (and us) that effective ministry requires balance: Jesus enables us to win the lost and then helps us nurture them into maturity. He had said to Peter, "And when you have turned back, strengthen your brothers" (Luke 22:32). Now we have three pictures of ministry: catching the fish, caring for the flock, and strengthening the family of God. Blessed are the balanced!

He Remembered His Opposition to the Cross (John 21:18–19)

When Jesus asked His disciples, "Who do you say I am?" it was Peter who answered for them, "You are the Christ, the Son of the living God" (Matt. 16:15–16). Then Jesus told them that they were going to Jerusalem where He would be arrested and crucified and be raised from the dead the third day. At that point Peter the rock became Peter the stumbling block, because Peter opposed the plan (vv. 21–28). Jesus made it very clear that Peter was playing right into the hands of Satan, who had already offered our Lord an earthly kingdom without a cross (Matt. 4:8–10). Jesus explained to all His disciples that each of them must take up a cross if they wanted to follow Him and be true disciples.

Having dealt with Peter's past, Jesus then turned to describe Peter's future. Jesus had restored Peter to fellowship; now He talked to Peter about his cross and what it would cost Peter to follow Him (John 21:18–19). The time would come when Peter would be crucified for his faith, but his death would bring glory to God. The old hymnist expressed it well:

> Must Jesus bear the cross alone,
> And all the world go free?
> No, there's a cross for every one,
> And there's a cross for me.
>
> The consecrated cross I'll bear,
> Till death shall set me free,
> And then go home my crown to wear,
> For there's a crown for me.[3]

In his second epistle, Peter referred to his impending death (2 Peter 1:12–15) and described it as taking down "the tent" and also as an "exodus" (the NIV reads "departure"). Peter may have had in mind his experience on the mount of transfiguration when he heard Jesus, Moses, and Elijah discussing the Lord's "exodus" that He would accomplish in Jerusalem (Luke 9:31). Peter suggested to Jesus that he be allowed to put up three tents for Him and the two prophets, but the Father interrupted Peter's speech and told him to listen to His Son (Matt. 17:4–8; Luke 9:33–36).

For the Christian believer, dying means that God takes down the temporary tent—the body—but promises us a permanent glorified body, "an eternal house in heaven, not built by human hands" (2 Cor. 5:1–5). Paul wasn't writing about a "mansion" in heaven; he was assuring believers that throughout eternity they wouldn't be disembodied spirits. They would be like Christ and have a glorified body. For Christians, death is truly an "exodus" as we're delivered from the bondage of mortal life and ushered into the presence of God, for to be "away from the body" means to be "at home with the Lord" (2 Cor. 5:6–9).

Did Peter recall how he had debated with Jesus about His announced death on a cross? Perhaps. But one thing is sure: He didn't argue when the Master told him he had a cross of his own in his future. When Jesus said, "Follow me!" (John 21:19), Peter got up and followed. The memories of past events—and even past failures—were no longer anchors to hold him back; they were rudders to guide him. Not only was Peter's fellowship restored but so also was his discipleship. And as he followed Jesus, he walked into one miracle after another.

ten

WHAT WILL WE GET?
HERE'S WHAT I'LL GIVE!

Acts 3:1–10

One day Peter and John were going up to the temple at
the time of prayer—at three in the afternoon. Now a man
crippled from birth was being carried to the temple gate
called Beautiful, where he was put every day to beg from
those going into the temple courts. When he saw Peter
and John about to enter, he asked them for money. Peter
looked straight at him, as did John. Then Peter said, "Look
at us!" So the man gave them his attention, expecting to
get something from them.

Then Peter said, "Silver or gold I do not have, but what
I have I give you. In the name of Jesus Christ of Nazareth,

walk." Taking him by the right hand, he helped him up, and instantly the man's feet and ankles became strong. He jumped to his feet and began to walk. Then he went with them into the temple courts, walking and jumping, and praising God. When all the people saw him walking and praising God, they recognized him as the same man who used to sit begging at the temple gate called Beautiful, and they were filled with wonder and amazement at what had happened to him.

*C*ontrary to popular religious mythology, Jesus never gave Peter the keys to the gates of heaven and assigned him the task of examining everybody who wanted to get in. The gates of heaven are never closed (Rev. 21:25), and we enter heaven because we've trusted the Savior and not because we've been approved by an apostle. Furthermore, Peter was commanded to use his "keys" on earth, not in heaven. By sharing the Word, Peter used "the keys of the kingdom" to open the door of faith to the Jews (Acts 2), the Samaritans (Acts 8), and the Gentiles (Acts 10).

Peter not only preached the Word, he also performed signs and wonders because the ability to do miracles was a part of his apostolic calling (Heb. 2:1–4; 2 Cor. 12:12). The first apostolic miracle recorded in the Book of Acts was the healing of a man over forty years old who had been lame from birth (Acts 3:2; 4:22). The account given by Dr. Luke presents a number of interesting contrasts that instruct us in the ways of the Lord and in some important aspects of Christian life and service.

Peter and John

The last time the New Testament recorded Peter and John walking together was when Jesus said, "Follow me!"

and reinstated Peter to his discipleship (John 21:19). Peter and John had been partners in the fishing business and had received their call to discipleship at the same time (Luke 5:1–11). It was Peter and John whom Jesus assigned to prepare the Passover before His crucifixion (Luke 22:7–13); and after His resurrection, Peter and John ran to investigate the empty tomb (John 20:1–10). When Jesus sent out the apostles two-by-two, it seems that He paired Peter with his brother Andrew (Matt. 10:1–4), but now it's Peter and John who went together to the temple (although they ended up in the prison) and ministered to a man in need.

Peter and John were both fishermen and had worked together in Capernaum, so they had much in common; but they appear to be different in their personalities. It's true that John and his brother James wanted to destroy a Samaritan village (Luke 9:51–56) and that Jesus nicknamed them "the sons of thunder" (Mark 3:17). But we don't usually think of John as a violent person. Whatever he may have been when he first began to follow Jesus, there's no question that John matured into a gracious servant of God. John became widely known as "the disciple whom Jesus loved" (John 13:23; 19:26; 20:2; 21:7, 20), and when he wrote his Gospel and epistles, his emphasis was on God's love for a lost world and our need to "love one another." John appears to have been a quiet man with a poetical and mystical outlook on life; quite different from the impulsive and inquisitive Simon Peter.

Jesus certainly had a diversity of men in His disciple band, but diversity is one of the strengths of the church, just as it is with the human body (1 Cor. 12–14). Christians get along with each other and work together because they are one in Christ, not because they have identical gifts and personalities. Believers who can work only with people whom they are like—and people they like—are in need of spiritual maturity. While it's true that Peter takes the lead in this miraculous event and does all the talking, John is still at his side and part of the miracle. John also went to jail with Peter and they stood together at the trial. "Two are better than one" (Eccles. 4:9), and these two lived and served as one. Such is the gracious ministry of the Lord when His people walk in the Spirit.

It's unfortunate that carnal competition and a selfish desire for uniformity have invaded the church and brought about divisions that have weakened our witness to the lost world. Some people follow human leaders—"I follow Paul . . . I follow Apollos . . . I follow Cephas." Others are so "spiritual" they reject all God-given leadership and only "follow Christ" (1 Cor. 1:12), which usually means following their own ideas and claiming they received them from Christ.

Peter and John are powerful examples to us of how two different personalities can walk together, work together, and witness together when they seek to honor Christ and depend on the Holy Spirit.

The Old and the New

On the Jewish clock, the third hour was nine in the morning, the sixth hour was noon, and the ninth hour was three in the afternoon. Peter and John were going to the temple to participate in the prayer service that accompanied the offering of the evening sacrifice. Although they belonged to Jesus Christ and had the Spirit of God dwelling within, they still associated with the Jewish worshipers in the temple. God accepted their worship no matter where they offered it, and the crowds in the temple provided the apostles with great opportunities for sharing their message.

The early church didn't separate from the temple and the synagogues until persecution drove them apart. In working out His wise plans on earth, the Lord rarely makes a sudden break with the past but generally makes His changes gradually. Even Israel's sudden exodus from Egypt was preceded by many weeks of divine judgments on Egypt and special preparation of God's people. The apostles were commanded to stay in Jerusalem and begin their witness there. Later the witness was shared with the Samaritans and the Gentiles, and eventually the church in Antioch became a second center along with Jerusalem for the spreading of the gospel. It didn't happen all at once.

Jesus has already made it clear that the new wine of the gospel couldn't be contained in the old wineskins of Judaism (Luke 5:36–39), but it would take time for the transition to occur. Peter and John had free access to the temple, but by the time you get to Acts 21–22, a mob in the temple tries to kill Paul, and the soldiers drag him out of the temple and shut the gates! If the old religious system had tried to absorb the new message and power of the gospel without being changed itself, both would have been destroyed. The Christian faith wasn't designed to be just another Jewish sect, for as Peter affirmed at the trial, "Salvation is found in no one else, for there is no other name under heaven given to men by which we must be saved" (Acts 4:12).

In the church today, we seem to forget that God wants to bring change in the midst of order and order in the midst of change. When the church adopts change just for the sake of change, it becomes novelty and weakens the witness. But when the church without compromise adapts itself to the needs and mind-set of people, change becomes an effective tool to reveal the life of the Spirit. The early church never wavered in its message, worship, or dependence on prayer and the Spirit, but it did alter its organization (Acts 6) and adapt its ministry as it moved into the Gentile world. If God's people are walking in the Spirit, there's no reason why there should be generational conflict over forms of worship and styles of music.

The Word of God and Prayer

Most people think of Peter primarily as a preacher of the Word, and indeed he was; but the secret of all the apostles' powerful public witness was their total dependence on prayer. Peter's Pentecost sermon was preceded by ten days of prayer, and there are nearly thirty references to prayer in the Book of Acts. Peter clearly expressed the priorities of the church leaders when he said, "[We] will give our attention to prayer and the ministry of the word" (Acts 6:4). Because they prayed and received God's Word, they were filled with the Holy Spirit and witnessed effectively.

We dare not separate these two powerful tools of the Spirit, because the Lord has ordained that they go together: "If anyone turns a deaf ear to the law, even his prayers are detestable" (Prov. 28:9). In the Word, God speaks to us and gives enlightenment; in prayer, we speak to God and receive enablement. Having the Word without prayer is like having light without power; but having prayer without the Word means power without light, and that creates zeal without knowledge. Blessed are the balanced.

Jesus told His disciples, "If you remain in me and my words remain in you, ask whatever you wish, and it will be given you" (John 15:7). In his ministry to Israel, Moses would meet with God in worship and prayer and then share with the people the Word he received from the Lord. This was also Samuel's approach to ministry: "As for me, far be it from me that I should sin against the Lord by failing to pray for you. And I will teach you the way that is good and right" (1 Sam. 12:23). You find this same pattern in the life of Daniel (Dan. 9:1–3) and even our Lord in His earthly ministry (Mark 1:35–39). Paul said to the Ephesian elders, "Now I commit you to God [that's prayer] and to the word of his grace, which can build you up and give you an inheritance among all those who are sanctified" (Acts 20:32).

"When people do not mind what God speaks to them in the Word, God as little minds what they say to Him in prayer." The Puritan author William Grunall wrote those words over three hundred years ago, but they apply to us today.

The Regular and the Special

Peter's going to the prayer meeting at the temple was a part of every devout Jewish man's regular schedule, but performing a miracle on a crippled beggar was something new and unusual. Life is made up of regularity and serendipity, and the disciplined believer never knows what a day will bring forth. We need regularity in life, because God wants things done "in a fitting and orderly way" (1 Cor. 14:40). The ordinary helps to prepare us for the extraordinary. But we also need to be open to the remarkable things the Lord may want to do for us and through us. Moses never expected to see a burning bush, but the experience changed the course of his life. David took a food parcel to his brothers in Saul's army and found out he was chosen by God to defeat a giant. Isaiah went to worship at the temple and found himself called to be a prophet. The one predictable thing about the believer's walk of faith is that—it's unpredictable!

The Beautiful Gate of the temple was actually a large ornate double door that took several men to open and close, and it guarded the entrance to the Court of the Women from the Court of the Gentiles. A helpless cripple was put daily before the gate because that was an ideal location for begging. (Giving alms to the poor was one of the required acts in Jewish worship.) So it was another "ordinary day" for the cripple. He would remain on the pavement all day, look as pitiful as possible, ask for money, and wait for his friends to pick him up and take him home. He never dreamed that the day would be any different, but it was!

We too must be open to the new things God wants to do for us. What begins as an ordinary, routine day may be interrupted by a miracle. That routine board meeting may turn into a "Beautiful Gate" experience, and there's no telling what might happen at a routine prayer meeting!

The Crowd and the Individual

Peter had recently preached to a large crowd of Jews and Jewish proselytes and had seen three thousand of them repent and turn to Christ. In one day, the Lord transformed him from a common fisherman into a powerful evangelist, and yet he had compassion for one poor beggar. This isn't always true of preachers who can move the multitudes; some of them have no time for individuals.

During the days when Jesus was ministering on earth, the disciples couldn't help but notice His concern for individuals in need. Jesus would speak to the multitudes that followed Him and then leave the crowd and minister personally to an unclean leper and the slave of a Roman soldier (Matt. 8:1–13). He helped a Samaritan woman find the living water (John 4), and He spoke to Zacchaeus the tax collector and brought him the gift of salvation (Luke 19:1–10). Even while dying on the cross, Jesus spoke to the condemned thief and brought him into the kingdom.

The disciples, however, weren't always that sensitive to the needs of the people who came to Jesus for help. More than once they stood in their way. They tried to keep parents from bringing their little ones to Jesus (Mark 10:13–16), and they suggested that Jesus send the hungry crowd home rather than feed them (Matt. 14:15). When the Canaanite woman begged Jesus to cure her demonized daughter, the disciples said, "Send her away, for she keeps crying out after us!" (Matt. 15:23). People can be pests, but even pesky people are candidates for miracles; and some of the problem people in our lives might turn out to become answers to our own problems.

God's work must not be planned and measured the way business leaders plan and measure their corporations. Why would Peter spend time with one beggar when he had opportunities to preach to great crowds and see thousands converted? Because one soul is precious to the Lord, and it's very like Jesus Christ to search for the one lost sheep. If the Creator of the universe pays attention when one bird falls to the ground (Matt. 10:29–31), shouldn't we be concerned about one beggar lying helpless on the ground? By ministering to that one beggar, Peter was given the opportunity to preach to another crowd *and two thousand more people trusted Christ* (Acts 4:4)! The church of Jesus Christ is changing the world one person at a time, so never underestimate the power of one changed life to help you reach the multitudes.

The Human and the Divine

The Lord could have healed the lame beggar when the man was at home, but He chose to use Peter as the human instrument of healing so that the miracle would then be identified with Jesus Christ and the gospel. The transformation of the man's body would bring glory to the name of Jesus Christ and give Peter opportunity to tell the crowd about the Savior. Each miracle the apostles performed was proof that Jesus was alive and working with His people. "Then the disciples went out and preached everywhere, and the Lord worked with them and confirmed his word by the signs that accompanied it" (Mark 16:20).

"The name of Jesus" is one of the repeated phrases in Acts 3–5, and it's a code phrase for all that Jesus is and does. Using "the name of Jesus" isn't a form of religious magic (see Acts 19:11–16) but a demonstration of faith in the power of Jesus. God healed the beggar because Peter had faith in the name of Jesus (Acts 3:6). Peter told the crowd that he and John hadn't done the miracle; it was done by Jesus whom the religious leaders had crucified (vv. 12–16). Since the Sadducees on the Jewish council didn't believe in the resurrection, they tried to silence Peter and John (Acts 4:1–3), but the two apostles made it clear that witnessing to the risen Christ was something they had to do (vv. 17–20).

God didn't ask for any help when He created the worlds, but when He put Adam into the Garden, He gave him work to do (Gen. 2:5, 15). God might have used angels, but He chose men and women, created in the image of God, to be the stewards of His creation. Science is simply thinking God's thoughts after Him and learning to harness for the good of humanity the principles God has built into the universe. Cooperate with these principles and you will build; oppose them and you will destroy.

So, whether it's planting a field for a harvest, digging a well for water, inventing a medication to cure disease, or providing food for a hungry child, God and people work together to get the job done. The same God who ordained the end— the healing of a cripple—also ordained the means to that end, which included the compassion, faith, hands, and voice of the apostle Peter. The crippled man at the Beautiful Gate met a stranger with beautiful feet who proclaimed the good news of deliverance (Isa. 52:7)! The power belonged to God, but the channel was a pair of humble believers who took time to share Jesus with a common beggar.

If God is going to speak to someone today, He will use a human voice or pen. He will manifest His love through human tears and sacrifices, and He will provide needs through human hands and hearts. If we make our possessions and ourselves available to the Lord and keep alert for the opportunities He gives us, we too can experience God's power and see Him do great things to the glory of Jesus.

Getting and Giving

After the rich young ruler turned down our Lord's terms for discipleship and went away grieved (Matt. 19:16–22), Peter said to Jesus, "We have left everything to follow you! What then will there be for us?" (v. 27). "What's in it for me?" is the question most people ask when called to make a sacrifice. But at the Beautiful Gate, Peter told the crippled man, "Silver or gold I do not have, but what I have I give you" (Acts 3:6). Peter had come a long way from "What will I get?" to "Whatever I have, I will give!"

Peter's question "What will we get?" reminds us that the Twelve weren't always interested in spiritual and eternal values, and this must have grieved the Lord. They argued over who was greatest in the kingdom, a topic that sometimes surfaced just after Jesus had spoken to them about His death on the cross. They tried to protect Jesus from interruptions and didn't realize that the interruptions were the ministry. They ended up building walls that isolated people instead of opening doors and inviting them to come to the Lord.

"Watch out! Be on your guard against all kinds of greed," said Jesus; "a man's life does not consist in the abundance of his possessions" (Luke 12:14). The apostle Paul quoted a parallel statement from our Lord that isn't recorded anywhere in the Gospel records: "It is more blessed to give than to receive" (Acts 20:35). It's blessed to receive, but it's more blessed to share what we receive. Peter couldn't give the beggar money because he didn't have any—and money wouldn't have met the poor man's real need anyway. Peter possessed something better than silver and gold: the power of Jesus Christ to change the man's life.

Too many believers are like the people in the church of Laodicea who boasted that they were rich and needed nothing, when actually they were "wretched, pitiful, poor, blind and naked" (Rev. 3:17). We forget that it's the "poor in spirit" who inherit God's kingdom and become rich in the things that matter most (Matt. 5:3), and that Jesus became poor so that we might become rich (2 Cor. 8:9). The paradox of Christian service is this: "poor, yet making many rich; having nothing, and yet possessing everything" (2 Cor. 6:10).

If you asked Peter what he did get because he left everything and followed Jesus, he would have replied, "His divine power has given us everything we need for life and godliness through our knowledge of him who called us by his own glory and goodness" (2 Peter 1:3).

What more could we want?

Popularity and Persecution

There was no doubt in anybody's mind that the lame man had been miraculously cured. "He jumped to his feet and began to walk. Then he went with them into the temple courts, walking and jumping, and praising God" (Acts 3:8; see Isa. 35:6). It's no wonder a crowd gathered and listened attentively to Peter's message. Even the members of the Sanhedrin said, "Everybody living in Jerusalem knows they have done an outstanding miracle, and we cannot deny it" (Acts 4:16). It's hard to deny a miracle when it's standing right there in the courtroom!

But miracles are a threat to people who don't know they need them, people like the Sadducees who rejected anything that had to do with spirits, angels, or the resurrection. As far as they were concerned, Jesus of Nazareth was still dead and His body had been stolen and hidden by His gullible disciples. The Sadducees had Peter and John arrested and kept in jail overnight, perhaps along with the crippled man who had been healed. First they put a miracle in jail, and then they closed their minds to what the miracle was saying to them. So much for blind "theology" and dead religious unbelief. The Sadducees had nothing to offer a poor cripple—or to anybody else, for that matter.

The arrest of Peter and John was the beginning of the persecution of Christians that's been going on until this day and that has robbed millions of Christian believers of liberty and even of life. "They will treat you this way because of my name," Jesus told His disciples in the upper room, "for they do not know the One who sent me" (John 15:21). Had Peter said to the cripple, "In the name of Abraham—or Moses—or King David—stand up and walk!" the Sanhedrin probably would never have interfered; but Peter used the name of Jesus, and that lit the fires of persecution. Tell a stranger that you're a Baptist, a Presbyterian, or even an atheist, and the conversation will go on without a problem; but tell the stranger that you're a Christian, and bring in the name of Christ, and you will face either a cold silence or a heated debate. Never mind. Just remember what Peter wrote to some persecuted saints:

> Dear friends, do not be surprised at the painful trial you are suffering, as though something strange were happening to you. But rejoice that you participate in the sufferings of Christ, so that you may be overjoyed when his glory is revealed. If you are insulted because of the name of Christ, you are blessed, for the Spirit of glory and of God rests on you.
>
> 1 Peter 4:12–14

Peter and Paul

We began our meditation considering Peter and John, but we can't ignore the apostle Paul, even though he wasn't on the scene or even a believer when this miracle occurred. But when we bring Paul into the picture, it helps us better understand the big picture of the Book of Acts and what the church should be doing today.

When the Holy Spirit called Dr. Luke to write the Book of Acts, He had several purposes in mind. In his Gospel, Dr. Luke wrote an accurate and inspired account of what Jesus began to do and teach during His life and ministry on earth (Luke 1:1–4; Acts 1:1–2). The Gospel of Luke is "a tale of two cities" and takes Jesus from Bethlehem to Jerusalem (Luke 9:31, 51–53; 13:22, 33; 17:11; 19:11, 28). In the Book of Acts, Dr. Luke carries the account further and tells how the church got from Jerusalem to Judea, then to Samaria, and to the uttermost parts of the earth, including Rome (Acts 1:8).

A second purpose behind the Book of Acts is an account of the growth of the church from its humble beginnings in Palestine. Dr. Luke gives us at least ten "summary statements" that describe this phenomenal growth (2:41, 47; 4:4; 5:14; 6:7; 9:31; 11:24; 12:24; 16:5; 19:20). The early church possessed none of the means of transportation and communication that we use today, yet they conquered the Roman Empire. What was their secret? Dr. Luke tells us: the Word of God, prayer, the power of the Spirit, and obedience to the will of God, even to the point of suffering and death.

Let me suggest a third purpose. Nowhere in Luke's historical account of the church does he say anything critical about a Roman centurion or Roman officers. He mentions Paul's Roman citizenship and that the Roman officers in Palestine found no fault in Paul and would have released him had he not appealed to Caesar. The Book of Acts could have been circulated anywhere in the Roman Empire without getting local Christians into trouble with Rome. The book is, as it were, an apologetic that defends Paul and the church from the false accusation that they were militantly opposed to Rome.

But the fourth purpose is the one that fits in with Peter's miracle of healing the lame man in the temple. The Holy Spirit led Dr. Luke to write Peter's story in the first part

(Acts 1–12) and Paul's story in the last part (Acts 13–28), but in no way did Luke rob Peter to pay Paul or Paul to pay Peter! Alas, the loyalty of some of the early congregations was divided between these two great leaders (the church at Corinth is an example, 1 Cor. 1:10–17), and this created problems in the churches. When you read Dr. Luke's inspired history, you discover that Peter and Paul had similar ministry experiences:

- Both healed men who were crippled from birth (Acts 3:1–8; 14:8–12)
- Both had to deal with satanic counterfeits (8:18–24; 13:4–12)
- Both were miraculously released from prison (12:1–10; 16:25–29)
- Both raised the dead (9:36–42; 20:7–12)
- Both were given special miracles to perform (5:15–16; 19:11)
- Both received remarkable visions from heaven (10:9–16; 9:1–8)

The Holy Spirit wanted to prevent the early church and the church throughout the ages from elevating one of God's choice servants above the other one. Both Peter and Paul were converted by trusting the same Savior, and they agreed on what they preached and taught. There is no "theology of Peter" that contradicts or questions the "theology of Paul." Both men were filled with the same Holy Spirit and proclaimed the same truth about Jesus. In fact, one of the last things Peter wrote in his second epistle was a clear statement that he and Paul agreed in their message (2 Peter 3:14–18).

The one thing we want to remember about this miracle is the evidence it gives of the spiritual maturity of Peter. He moved from "What shall we get?" to "What I have, I will give you." He had discovered that Christians get more blessing out of giving than out of receiving.

eleven

ME AND MY SHADOW

Acts 5:12-16

The apostles performed many miraculous signs and wonders among the people. And all the believers used to meet
together in Solomon's Colonnade. No one else dared join
them, even though they were highly regarded by the people. Nevertheless, more and more men and women believed in the Lord and were added to their number. As a
result, people brought the sick into the streets and laid
them on beds and mats so that at least Peter's shadow might
fall on some of them as he passed by. Crowds gathered also
from the towns around Jerusalem, bringing their sick and
those tormented by evil spirits, and all of them were healed.

*P*eople who lived in Bible lands long ago paid far more attention to shadows than we do in our modern world. They told time by the shadows (2 Kings 20:9–10), but we simply glance at the clock on the wall or the watch on our wrist. When the sun was high, ancient eastern peoples sought for a cool place in the shadows. We turn on the air-conditioning. Ancient people knew that shadows could hide danger and trouble, but all we do is turn on the lights or pull out a flashlight; and if something approaches the house, special "sentry lights" come on automatically. Eastern peoples especially saw shadows as images of the brevity and swiftness of life. "My days are like the evening shadow," wrote the psalmist (Ps. 102:11). And suffering Job lamented, "Man born of woman is of few days and full of trouble. He springs up like a flower and withers away; like a fleeting shadow, he does not endure" (Job 14:1–2). Of course, the safest place in the world is "in the shadow of the Almighty" (Ps. 91:1). David wrote, "I will take refuge in the shadow of your wings until the disaster has passed" (Ps. 57:1). He may have been referring to the wings of the cherubim in the Holy of Holies.

But perhaps the most unusual reference to shadows in Scripture is Acts 5:15: "People brought the sick into the streets and laid them on beds and mats so that at least Peter's shadow might fall on some of them as he passed by." Imagine being the possessor of a healing shadow!

The Intangible

A shadow is the product of a solid body standing in the way of a ray of light. You can see a shadow and even measure its length and width, but you can't feel it, weigh it, or discover how thick it is. Shadows are intangible. When you say, "I don't have the shadow of a doubt," you're confessing to being as close to certainty as fallible humans can get. Yet God used Peter's intangible shadow to accomplish some very tangible results.

But did He? Were those sick people actually healed, or was the whole thing only a demonstration of superstitious faith? The text doesn't affirm that the sick people were healed, but from the way the narrative is written, we assume that miracles did actually occur. The Acts 5 narrative is something like Matthew's report of Peter catching the fish with the coin in its mouth: The text doesn't describe the event, but we assume that it happened. Otherwise, why record it? If God hadn't used Peter's shadow to bring healing to the sick, the people would soon have stopped burdening themselves with the task of carrying the sick out to the streets.

The apostles were doing many miracles and wonders among the people (5:12) so that the unbelieving Jews held the church in very high regard and many of them trusted in Christ. It appears that it was these new believers who kept bringing the afflicted people to be healed. The reports of the healings attracted people from the towns around Jerusalem (v. 16), and this is the first recorded instance in the Book of Acts of apostolic miracles for people from outside the Holy City. Peter's shadow was reaching out farther and farther!

God uses a variety of instruments to accomplish His work, but the power is always from Him. In fact, He loves to use tools that the world laughs at and rejects. When the Lord wanted to found the Hebrew nation, He chose Abraham and Sarah, a couple who were too old to have children. All Moses had in his hand was a shepherd's rod, but God used it to begin His campaign against the Egyptian nation. God gave Gideon and his small army torches and pitchers to use in attacking the horde of Midianites, and Gideon won the battle (Judg. 7). All David had to fight with was a sling and some stones, but he defeated a giant. Our Lord once used mud to give a blind man sight (John 9), and now He was using the shadow of a common Jewish fisherman to bring healing to the people. If their faith was tinged with superstition, so was the faith of the woman healed of her hemorrhage (Matt. 9:20–22) and the faith of the multitudes who wanted to touch the hem of Jesus' garment (Mark 6:53–56). God accepts and encourages even the weakest faith.

Peter's shadow is an encouragement to those of us who too often feel inadequate and ill-equipped to serve the Master. It's also a rebuke to those who like to take the credit for what the Lord has done through them. It does us good to remember what we were when the Lord called us and to acknowledge what He has accomplished in spite of us!

> Not many of you were wise by human standards; not many were influential; not many were of noble birth. But God chose the foolish things of the world to shame the wise; God chose the weak things of the world to shame the strong. He chose the lowly things of this world and the despised things—and the things that are not—to nullify the things that are, so that no one may boast before him.
>
> 1 Corinthians 1:26–29

The Incidental

These miracles didn't take place at special meetings organized by the apostles but along the streets as Peter walked through the city. As he walked, Peter became a dispenser of miracles, a good example for us to follow. We may not be able to heal broken bodies, but we can help heal broken hearts and damaged lives as we go through the day and share the love and truth of Jesus.

The American poet Henry Wadsworth Longfellow tried to encourage us when he wrote this stanza in "A Psalm of Life":

> Lives of great men all remind us
> We can make our lives sublime,
> And, departing, leave behind us
> Footprints on the sands of time.

Few people, however, can honestly call themselves "great," and what good are footprints on the sand to people who can't walk? The sentiment is beautiful, but where is the power to change lives? In contrast, wherever Peter walked in his daily life, he left miracles behind and brought Jesus Christ into the lives of other people. That's what Christian living is all about—walking through life and leaving miracles behind.

If you had followed Abraham day after day in his journey of faith, you would have noticed that he left behind wells that he dug, trees that he planted, and altars that he built. The people coming after him would have found refreshing water and shade as well as places for spiritual worship, not a bad contribution from an elderly husband and wife! Had you followed the people of Israel during their forty years of wandering, you would have passed hundreds of gravesites that they left behind. Their journey was one long funeral march as the unbelieving older generation died and made way for the new generation to enter the Promised Land.

Some of our greatest contributions to the happiness and welfare of others may seem purely incidental, but God can use them just the same. In fact, it's often the incidental and hidden ministries that bring Him the most glory. During a devotional talk to a ministry staff, I mentioned the name of a book that had been a great help to me in my early Christian life, and one of the men in the meeting bought a copy. He later phoned me and told me that reading the book had changed his life. In a casual conversation with a friend, the Lord used his words to help me make an important decision, the consequences of which I still benefit from today. Never underestimate the power of your shadow in the so-called incidental experiences of life.

The Indispensable

The South African author Laurens van der Post tells in one of his books that the indigenous people of his land have a unique way of expressing their confidence in an individual. They say, "Indeed, you throw a shadow." In other words, the person isn't somebody you can "see through," somebody who is without substance and is mere illusion. People you can't see through are solid individuals who are real enough to cast shadows.[1] Peter threw a shadow because Peter was a real man and a real Christian.

After the Civil War, an ambitious insurance company offered to pay Robert E. Lee $10,000 a year if he would become the "titular head" of their company. He refused the offer and wrote, "Excuse me, sir; I cannot consent to receive pay for services I do not render." He was a man of integrity, a man who had a shadow.

When the prophet Isaiah wanted to describe faithful leaders, he wrote, "Each man will be like a shelter from the wind and a refuge from the storm, like streams of water in the desert and the shadow of a great rock in a thirsty land" (Isa. 32:2). Peter "the rock" qualified, for he had a shadow that proved he was real, a person of integrity. The American Management Association sponsored a study to determine what qualities managers most valued in their leaders. When the results were in, the top three qualities were integrity, competence, and the ability to lead and give direction.[2]

Integrity is indispensable for character, conduct, and service. However, we live at a time when the popular mind separates ability and integrity and people ask, "What difference does it make how our leaders live so long as they get the job done?" In other words, leaders don't need values and character; all they need is professional expertise and the ability to get things done. But this is saying that God wasted a great deal of time transforming Moses the prince into Moses the prophet, David the shepherd into David the king, and Simon the sand into Peter the rock. People with integrity are people with values that have been refined and polished on the battlefield of testing and temptation. Leaders without integrity are but "see-through" people, masters of manipulation and illusion, and they and their work will both be exposed for what they are—cheap imitations of the real thing.

The Incompatible

The person whose shadow produces miracles is going to have enemies, and Peter was no exception. "Then the high priest and all his associates, who were members of the party of the Sadducees, were filled with jealousy. They arrested the apostles and put them in the public jail" (Acts 5:17–18). It was the same unbelieving crowd that had arrested Peter and John after the healing of the crippled beggar (Acts 4:1–3). These religious leaders could skillfully argue their theology and "prove" there was no resurrection of the dead, but they weren't able to do miracles. Their "scientific" approach to life and death had been exposed as foolish by what Jesus taught, and then it had been utterly destroyed by His resurrection. Every miracle that the apostles did was proof that Jesus was alive and the kingdom had come. The Lord answered the opposition of the Sadducees by sending an angel who let the apostles out of jail.

From the very beginning, the message and ministry of the church were incompatible with the traditional religion that held the Jewish people in bondage. Everything about the church is countercultural, and when that ceases to be true, the church starts to drift from its true message and mission. Instead of indicting the world and its evil, the church begins to imitate the world and become intimate with it. Before long, you can't distinguish between the world and the church.

G. Campbell Morgan said that the church did the most for the world when the church was the least like the world, and he was right. However, Paul's admonition "Do not conform any longer to the pattern of this world" (Rom. 12:2) goes unheeded by many professed believers today. As a result, the church is largely ignored by the world or else used by it to promote its own values and agenda. It's difficult to tell a "religious trade show" from its secular counterparts.

When the Lord raises up dedicated Christian leaders who cast shadows, their biggest enemies are those of their own household. Powerless religion doesn't know what to do with a maverick like Peter, who goes about demonstrating that Jesus Christ is alive. The fact that the apostles just didn't fit with Caiaphas and his crowd is to their credit, and God honored them for their stand. Caiaphas and the council may have had authority, but Peter and his friends had power that no political or religious authority could stop.

Peter wasn't interested in being accepted by or popular in the world, nor should the church be today. Peter had heard Jesus say, "I have come to bring fire on the earth" (Luke 12:49), and "If they persecuted me, they will persecute you also" (John 15:20). He also heard the Lord say, "What is highly valued among men is detestable in God's sight" (Luke 16:15), and he believed it. To Peter and the other apostles, courting the friendship and approval of the world was contrary to everything that Jesus taught and for which He died. Paul agreed with them when he wrote, "May I never boast except in the cross of our Lord Jesus Christ, through which the world has been crucified to me, and I to the world" (Gal. 6:14). Neither Peter nor Paul wanted to shine in the world. They wanted God's glory to shine through them and their shadows to bless others.

Bishop William Quayle of the Methodist Church wrote, "We have not religion in its totality until our shadows become converted."

The church today needs more converted shadows.

twelve

PETER, AT YOUR SERVICE

Acts 9:32–43

As Peter traveled about the country, he went to visit the saints in Lydda. There he found a man named Aeneas, a paralytic who had been bedridden for eight years. "Aeneas," Peter said to him, "Jesus Christ heals you. Get up and take care of your mat." Immediately Aeneas got up. All those who lived in Lydda and Sharon saw him and turned to the Lord.

In Joppa there was a disciple named Tabitha (which, when translated, is Dorcas), who was always doing good and helping the poor. About that time she became sick and died, and her body was washed and placed in an upstairs room. Lydda was near Joppa; so when the disciples heard that Peter was in Lydda, they sent two men to him and urged him, "Please come at once!"

Peter went with them, and when he arrived he was taken upstairs to the room. All the widows stood around him, crying and showing him the robes and other clothing that Dorcas had made while she was still with them.

Peter sent them all out of the room; then he got down on his knees and prayed. Turning toward the dead woman, he said, "Tabitha, get up." She opened her eyes, and seeing Peter she sat up. He took her by the hand and helped her to her feet. Then he called the believers and the widows and presented her to them alive. This became known all over Joppa, and many people believed in the Lord. Peter stayed in Joppa for some time with a tanner named Simon.

*W*hen I was a seminary student, our New Testament instructor encouraged us to "think through" each book of the New Testament regularly so that we would be able to identify the key event in each chapter. We would say to ourselves, "Acts chapter 1—choosing a new apostle. Acts chapter 2—Pentecost. Acts chapter 3—healing the crippled beggar," and so on. Of course, when we got to Acts chapter 9, we said, "The conversion and call of Paul." We casually ignored the fact that Peter was still very active and that the chapter recorded two miracles that God enabled him to perform: the healing of Aeneas and the raising of Dorcas from the dead. Remembering these miracles could help us learn some important lessons about ministry.

Courage

These were not easy days for the church. Saul of Tarsus, the outstanding young Pharisee of his day (Gal. 1:14), was persecuting the church so severely that many of the saints in Jerusalem left the city and scattered to safer places. However, instead of destroying the church, the persecution only gave the gospel message a wider hearing (Acts 8:1–8). God's people are like seed, and when they're scattered and take root, they produce a harvest.

Dr. Luke tells us that during the persecution, the apostles remained in Jerusalem, and some people have criticized them for that. "It was time to get the message out," the critics argue, "and the apostles should have been on the move!" But it took a great deal of courage for these men to remain in the place of danger, doing their job and caring for the infant church. Instead of criticizing the apostles, we ought to admire them for risking their lives for the people of God.

Philip the deacon/evangelist was directed by the Lord to minister in Samaria, and there he preached the gospel to people who had no great love for the Jews. When the Assyrians conquered the northern kingdom of Israel seven centuries before, they had integrated the Jewish population with Gentile people from other nations they had defeated, and this produced a hybrid people with a hybrid religion. Orthodox Jews wanted nothing to do with either the Samaritans or their religion, so for a Jewish evangelist to preach the gospel message in Samaria took courage indeed. Philip was only following the Lord's agenda stated in Acts 1:8. The church had evangelized Jerusalem and Judea, and now it was time for a harvest in Samaria.

At a time when it was perilous for Christian leaders to be traveling, Peter and John followed up Philip's ministry and visited Samaria. They imparted the gift of the Spirit to the new believers there, and this healed the long-standing separation between the Jews and the Samaritans. Peter would then minister to the Gentiles (Acts 10–11), and then Paul would take the message to "the uttermost part of the earth." God had His agenda and His timetable, and whether the apostles remained in Jerusalem or visited other areas, they were obeying God's will. Instead of criticizing them, we ought to be imitating them!

Sometimes we focus so much on Peter's denial that we forget his courage. When Jesus was arrested in the Garden, Peter's zeal was misguided, but his courage was very evident. He preached Christ boldly at Pentecost and also afterward. Twice he had been put in jail, and once he had been beaten and warned to keep quiet, so you can hardly label him a coward. It was dangerous for him to remain in Jerusalem and even more dangerous to go with John to Samaria, but Peter was a faithful servant of God who took his ministry seriously.

It's possible for a man or woman to cultivate a ministry of comfort and convenience, but that isn't the kind of ministry the Spirit blesses or that Christ will reward in heaven. Only a ministry of sacrifice and service will glorify the Lord on that day when God transforms scars into medals and crosses into crowns. When he was a young disciple, Peter opposed Jesus going to the cross because he could see no connection between the suffering of the Master and the glorious kingdom of the Messiah (Matt. 16:21–23). But Peter soon learned that suffering for Christ always leads to glory, and when he wrote his first epistle, that was one of his major themes. "If you are insulted because of the name of Christ, you are blessed, for the Spirit of glory and of God rests on you" (1 Peter 4:14).

Let's be steadfast in the places of God's appointment and busy in the activities of God's choosing, no matter how difficult or dangerous. As Dr. V. Raymond Edman used to tell the students at Wheaton College, "It's always too soon to quit."

Cooperation

After Saul the persecutor was converted, the Lord gave the church a temporary relief from suffering, and this led to a period of exceptional growth (Acts 9:31). It also meant that the believers in Jerusalem were safe from harassment and arrest so that their spiritual leaders could help the saints in other places. After ministering in Samaria, Philip went to Gaza where he led an Ethiopian official to faith in Christ (Acts 8:26–38). Then Philip was taken to Azotus, about twenty miles northeast of Gaza, and "traveled about, preaching the gospel in all the towns until he reached Caesarea" (Acts 8:40). This meant he must have evangelized in Azotus, Jamnia, Lydda, Joppa, and Antiparis before reaching Caesarea, where years later we find him living with his daughters and entertaining Paul and his party (Acts 21:7–9).

When Jesus ministered in Samaria and reaped a splendid harvest (John 4), He said to His disciples, "Thus the saying 'One sows and another reaps' is true. I sent you to reap what you have not worked for. Others have done the hard work, and you have reaped the benefits of their labor" (John 4:37–38). Jesus may have been referring to the work of John the Baptist and his disciples, who possibly had preached in that area. Peter must have recalled those words of Jesus as he responded to calls to Lydda, where he healed Aenaes, and Joppa, where he raised Dorcas from the dead. He was entering into the faithful labors of Philip the evangelist, otherwise there might have been no believers in those cities.

It's unfortunate when the laborers in the harvest field are motivated by a spirit of competition and comparing spiritual gifts or the size of the harvest or the amount of work that they did. Aren't all faithful laborers a part of the harvest, and isn't Jesus Christ the Lord of the harvest who alone deserves all the glory? At least that's what Paul wrote to the church at Corinth:

> What, after all, is Apollos? And what is Paul? Only servants, through whom you came to believe—as the Lord has assigned to each his task. I planted the seed, Apollos watered it, but God made it grow. So neither he who plants

nor he who waters is anything, but only God, who makes things grow. The man who plants and the man who waters have one purpose, and each will be rewarded according to his own labor.

1 Corinthians 3:5–8

As Jesus told His disciples in Samaria, "One sows and another reaps."

To change the image but not the subject, Peter was a fisherman who knew the importance of teamwork. Commercial fishermen worked with large nets that one man could not effectively handle alone. This is why Peter, Andrew, James, and John were partners in the fishing business, and all of them learned to be partners in fishing for lost sinners. There are many boats, nets, and faithful fishermen on the sea of life, and the Lord can use all of them.

The longer I minister, the more I marvel at the wonderful way the Holy Spirit uses the labors of many people to accomplish the will of God. I trusted Christ at a Youth for Christ rally where Billy Graham was the speaker, but behind my decision that night was a great deal of teamwork. Starting with the people who organized the rally, consider also the influence of home and family and the ministry of Sunday school teachers and Vacation Bible School workers. God also used the prayers of concerned pastors and relatives, the ministry of Christian radio, the Bible verses I had memorized, and even the songs I had learned to sing in Sunday school and church. And that doesn't include everybody!

"For we are God's fellow workers" (1 Cor. 3:9), which suggests that we are also working with each other to accomplish what God wants to accomplish. Nobody's ministry is insignificant, and everybody's ministry is important and necessary. There are no "small" places and there are no "big" ministers.

Commission

The first time Jesus sent out His apostles, He gave them power for ministry and authority to minister (Matt. 10). They served as the Lord's commissioned agents and not as freelance, self-appointed workers. His mandate was, "As you go, preach this message: 'The kingdom of heaven is near.' Heal the sick, raise the dead, cleanse those who have leprosy, drive out demons. Freely you have received, freely give" (Matt. 10:7–8). In spite of his failures, Peter's power and authority hadn't been taken from him, and he went forth to serve the Lord and His people.

And Jesus had given Peter a second commission: "And when you have turned back, strengthen your brothers" (Luke 22:32). We read in Acts 9 about only two special miracles, but Peter ministered in many ways to many people as he "traveled about the country" in the maritime plain (Acts 9:32). William Barclay translates that phrase, "In the course of a tour of the whole area." Peter was engaged in an "apostolic visitation" to help establish the new converts, win the lost, and assist the local assemblies in solving their problems and making good use of their opportunities. What a privilege it would have been to sit under Simon Peter's ministry and hear him talk about Jesus!

There was a third commission: "Feed my lambs. . . . Take care of my sheep. . . . Feed my sheep" (John 21:15–17). Peter the fisherman was also Peter the shepherd, and his ministry had to be motivated by his love for Jesus Christ. It may be easy to love a cuddly little lamb, but it isn't easy to take care of an old stubborn sheep! Only our love for Christ can keep us on the job when the going is difficult.

Peter had to show the shepherds of the local flocks how to lead the people into the green pastures of the Word, how to protect them from predators, and how to help them build unity and harmony in the flock.

> Be shepherds of God's flock that is under your care, serving as overseers—not because you must, but because you are willing, as God wants you to be; not greedy for money, but eager to serve; not lording it over those entrusted to you, but being examples to the flock. And when the Chief Shepherd appears, you will receive the crown of glory that will never fade away.
>
> 1 Peter 5:2–4

Without faithful shepherds, the flocks will scatter and become vulnerable to the enemies that surround them. Jesus loves His flock and wants His love to flow through the ministries of faithful undershepherds who will tenderly care for them. Shepherds must do more than teach the flock, which seems to be the major emphasis today. Like Jesus, they must know their sheep by name, understand their personal needs, spend time with them, and seek to lead them into maturity (John 10). The hireling serves as long as he is paid for working, but when there's danger abroad, he forsakes the flock and protects himself.

Somewhere we have lost the biblical image of the church as a flock and the minister as a shepherd (which is what *pastor* means). I heard about one minister who forbade his congregation to call him "pastor" because he didn't see himself as a shepherd. What kind of a calling and gifting did he have? Was he called at all?

Command

Lydda was located about twenty-five miles northwest of Jerusalem, and while ministering there, Peter got acquainted with Aeneas, "a paralytic who had been bedridden for eight years" (Acts 9:33). The name Aeneas means "praise," but it appeared that he had little for which to be thankful. If you remember the classics you may have read in high school or college, you'll recognize "Aeneas" as the name of Virgil's hero in his epic poem about the Trojan War, *The Aeneid.* Perhaps the Aeneas Peter met in Lydda was a hero in patience and courage, but he was far from being a great conqueror.

The living Christ was still at work on earth through His people, so by faith Peter drew upon His resurrection power and helped Aeneas. "Jesus Christ heals you," said Peter. "Get up and take care of your mat" (v. 34). Peter may have remembered the paralytic whom Jesus healed in Capernaum, the man whose four friends let him down through an opening in the roof (Mark 2:1–12). It's possible that it was in Peter's house that the miracle took place. Jesus said to the man, "I tell you, get up, take your mat and go home" (Mark 2:11). In both instances, the men were instantly healed and obeyed the Lord's command.

Paralysis robs a person of the enjoyments and the achievements of life. Paralyzed people must be assisted in everything they do, and perhaps the saints in Lydda took turns ministering to this helpless man. I don't want to turn this miracle into an allegory, but we must face the fact that there are people today who suffer from paralysis of the will and of the spirit. Some are unable to stop destructive habits; others lack the power to stay on the job and be productive; many can't confront problems and solve them; and still others lack the discipline they need to build a balanced and wholesome life. All of them need Jesus.

The plight of Aeneas must have been known widely, because when he was healed, everybody heard about it and talked about it. Like Lazarus whom Jesus raised from the dead (John 11:45; 12:17–19), Aeneas was a living and walking sermon! "All those who lived in Lydda and Sharon saw him and turned to the Lord" (Acts 9:35). That made his eight years of pain and trouble worthwhile! It was a repeat of the lesson of the cripple at the Beautiful Gate of the temple: Reach one and you will reach a multitude.

Joppa was situated about ten miles northwest of Lydda, and when the believers in Joppa heard about this miracle, they immediately sent for Peter to come quickly. Their beloved "resident seamstress" had died, and this was a great loss to the church. Her name was Dorcas (that's Greek) or Tabitha (which is Aramaic), both of which mean "gazelle." She had the gift of mercy and kept her needle busy as she made garments for the poor. She was always doing good and always helping the poor, which could well be a description of Jesus when He was ministering on earth. In almost every church, there are people like Dorcas who dedicate themselves to the Lord and use their gifts and abilities to serve Him. What would we do without them!

This raises the difficult question, "Why does God permit dedicated and useful saints to suffer and die?" In my own pastoral ministry, I recall how the loss of devoted men and women—teachers, elders, helpers—left empty places in the church that weren't easy to fill. There are mysteries here that can't be solved in a few paragraphs, and we must never question the sovereign will of God. Sometimes in losing one worker the church has opportunity to challenge other workers, and they respond to the challenge and thereby strengthen the church. The loss of a godly leader certainly motivates others to follow the example and seek to minister to the flock.

There was no question that the death of Dorcas touched the congregation deeply, especially the people whom she had helped. It does us all good to ask, "If I were taken home, would I really be missed and why? Would the witness I left behind truly honor the Lord and touch the hearts of His people?"

In the city of Jerusalem, people were usually buried within twenty-four hours of their death, but away from Jerusalem, the dead might lie in state for as long as three days. The Jews did not embalm the body; they washed it, dressed it, applied spices, and placed it in an upper room. What Peter did in that upper room reminds us of what Jesus did when He raised the daughter of Jairus from the dead (Mark 5:40–43). Peter put everybody out, prayed, spoke to the woman, and took her by the hand. In the Aramaic language, Peter said, "Tabitha cumi—Tabitha, get up!" Jesus had said to the little girl, "Talitha koum—little girl, get up."

It's too bad some of the Sadducees from Jerusalem hadn't been there to witness this resurrection! But the word spread and many people trusted Christ because of what God had done for Dorcas. Before long, Dorcas was back to her ministry, and no doubt she never tired of telling visitors how Jesus had raised her from the dead.

Continuity

In the life of a dedicated believer, as well as in the life of a Spirit-led church, no event is an isolated accident. Whatever happens is part of a larger scenario that God has planned for His people. Peter's ministry in Joppa brought life to Dorcas and comfort to her many friends, but much more was involved. There was another blessed by-product from this miracle: *it got Peter to Joppa.* In heeding the call of the church at Joppa, Peter unconsciously prepared himself to receive a special vision there from the Lord, a vision that would lead to the door of faith being opened to the Gentiles (Acts 10). Jonah was called to take God's message to the Gentiles, but he disobeyed orders and sailed in the opposite direction, stopping at Joppa on his way to escape (Jonah 1:1–3). Peter tarried at Joppa, saw a marvelous vision, and obeyed what God told him to do (Acts 10).

When he wrote the Book of Acts, Dr. Luke didn't just string together one incident after another. Led by the Holy Spirit, he wrote the story of the spread of the gospel from Jerusalem to Judea, then to Samaria, and now to the towns on the maritime plain between Judea and Samaria and the Mediterranean Sea. The fact that Peter was living in Joppa with a tanner indicates that his orthodox Jewish ways were starting to disappear, because tanning leather was an unclean occupation, and to live with a tanner meant to become unclean. He would soon learn that he shouldn't call the Gentiles "unclean" because they too could be saved by the grace of God.

Through this vision, God prepared Peter to visit the household of Cornelius, a devout Roman centurion who was searching for eternal life. Peter never got to finish the sermon he preached to Cornelius and his relatives and friends! When he got to the essence of the gospel—"everyone who believes in him receives forgiveness of sins through his name" (Acts 10:43)—his listeners heard that promise, believed, were saved, and immediately received the gift of the Holy Spirit!

When Peter returned to Jerusalem, some of the legalistic Jewish believers criticized him for going to a Gentile house, preaching to Gentiles, and eating with them. Peter not only defended himself successfully before these legalists, but he ably defended the gospel before the entire council at Jerusalem (Acts 15:1–11). He didn't say, "The Gentiles are saved just as we Jews are," but, "We Jews are saved just as the Gentiles are—by faith in Jesus Christ!"

If Peter had not tarried in Joppa and been obedient to the heavenly vision, where would the Gentiles be today?

thirteen

Waking Up to Miracles!

Acts 12:1–19

So Peter was kept in prison, but the church was earnestly praying to God for him.

The night before Herod was to bring him to trial, Peter was sleeping between two soldiers, bound with two chains, and sentries stood guard at the entrance. Suddenly an angel of the Lord appeared and a light shone in the cell. He struck Peter on the side and woke him up. "Quick, get up!" he said, and the chains fell off Peter's wrists.

Then the angel said to him, "Put on your clothes and sandals." And Peter did so. "Wrap your cloak around you and follow me," the angel told him. Peter followed him out of the prison, but he had no idea that what the angel was doing was really happening; he thought he was seeing a vision. They passed the first and second guards and came to the iron gate leading to the city. It opened for them by itself, and they went through it. When they had walked the length of one street, suddenly the angel left him.

Then Peter came to himself and said, "Now I know without a doubt that the Lord sent his angel and rescued me from Herod's clutches and from everything the Jewish people were anticipating."

When this had dawned on him, he went to the house of Mary the mother of John, also called Mark, where many people had gathered and were praying. Peter knocked at the outer entrance, and a servant girl named Rhoda came to answer the door. When she recognized Peter's voice, she was so overjoyed she ran back without opening it and exclaimed, "Peter is at the door!"

"You're out of your mind," they told her. When she kept insisting that it was so, they said, "It must be his angel."

But Peter kept on knocking, and when they opened the door and saw him, they were astonished. Peter motioned with his hand for them to be quiet and described how the Lord had brought him out of prison. "Tell James and the brothers about this," he said, and then he left for another place.

Acts 12:5–17

Except for a cameo appearance at the Jerusalem Conference (Acts 15), Peter steps out of the Book of Acts in chapter 12 and makes way for Paul. He says very little in this chapter, only a quiet reflection to himself (v. 11) and a simple instruction to the saints in Mary's house (v. 17)—"and then he left for another place." What other place? We don't know, nor is it important that we know. What is important is that we learn the truths that are revealed in this prison experience of Peter and apply them in our own Christian walk.

This is the third time Peter has been in confinement. He was in jail with John (Acts 4:1–4) and then later with the other apostles (5:17–18), but the experience described in chapter 12 is different from the other two. For one thing, Peter's imprisonment did not follow the great victories that preceded the other imprisonments; rather, it followed a great tragedy—the martyrdom of James. Also, this time Peter was alone, without the encouragement of the other apostles. In his earlier experiences, all they had to face was a trial and perhaps a beating; but this time, Peter was facing execution. The apostles were quickly delivered from the first two confinements, but in this one, Peter was kept in prison at least a week. No two testings are exactly the same, but the resources of God never change.

In this chapter, Dr. Luke gives us a study in contrasts and helps us understand how to deal with the trials that are bound to arise when we faithfully serve the Lord.

Two Enemies

The man on the throne was Herod Agrippa I, grandson of Herod the Great, who killed the babies in Bethlehem. He was also the nephew of Herod Antipas, who ordered John the Baptist beheaded, so he belonged to quite a violent family! This branch of the Herod family was Edomite in ancestry, descendants of Esau, who wanted to kill his brother Jacob. (James is another form of the name Jacob.) It was the old familiar feud between the carnal and the spiritual that shows up frequently in Scripture: Isaac and Ishmael, Jacob and Esau, Joseph and his brothers, David and Saul. But even more, Herod Agrippa's attack on the church was evidence of the conflict between Christ and Satan, God's children and Satan's children, that's been going ever since God declared war on Satan in Genesis 3:15. It started with Cain killing Abel, and it will climax with Satan and

Antichrist being thrown into the lake of fire (Rev. 19:20; 20:10). Whether we like it or not, every Christian believer is involved in a vast cosmic conflict and is either fighting with Christ or against Him.

Herod's desire wasn't to please the Lord but to please the people, so he killed James and imprisoned Peter. Herod was a proud man who wanted to be treated like a god (Acts 12:20–23). That was Lucifer's ambition: "I will make myself like the Most High" (Isa. 14:14). The apostle John summarized "the world" in three vivid phrases: "the cravings of sinful man, the lust of his eyes and the boasting of what he has and does" (1 John 2:16). Herod was a proud man who used his authority to please himself, but when God wanted to take him off the scene, all He needed was a few worms to eat out his viscera, and the king was dead.

We need to remind ourselves that our battle is not against the people and organizations that we can see but "against the rulers, against the authorities, against the powers of this dark world and against the spiritual forces of evil in the heavenly realm" (Eph. 6:12). Everything people have seen in *Star Wars* and *Star Trek* is playground stuff compared with the cosmic conflict now going on between Satan and the church. The trouble is, many of God's people don't even realize that there is a fierce battle going on, and their ignorance is making it easier for the enemy to win.

Our enemy isn't flesh and blood, but Satan uses human beings to get his work done in this world. Our task is to exercise discernment and know where the enemy is at work and then use the spiritual weapons Christ has given us to expose him and defeat him. We must wear the armor (Eph. 6:10–18) and use the Word of God and prayer to overcome the wiles of the devil. Herod Agrippa is dead, but people like him are legion, and Satan is using them to oppose the work of Jesus Christ. Jesus and Satan will be in conflict until Christ returns and claims the kingdoms of this world for Himself and His people. No wonder Peter wrote, "Be self-controlled and alert.

Your enemy the devil prowls around like a roaring lion look-ing for someone to devour" (1 Peter 5:8).

Two Servants

There were thousands of believers in Jerusalem, yet Herod arrested Peter and James, the brother of John; and like our Lord's arrest, it took place during Passover season. Satan prefers to attack effective Christian leaders, which ought to encourage us to pray faithfully for the high-profile people in churches and parachurch ministries who are on the cutting edge of the Lord's work. If leaders fall, entire ministries could fall with them. Peter and James were Spirit-filled leaders who were attacking Satan's strongholds and delivering his slaves into the victory of Christ. No won-der the enemy was after them!

We can't explain why James was executed and Peter res-cued, but we know God makes no mistakes. There are, how-ever, some factors to consider. On three different occasions, our Lord took Peter, James, and John with Him for a spe-cial experience: on the mount of transfiguration (Matt. 17:1–8), in the home of Jairus (Luke 8:51–56), and in the Garden of Gethsemane (Mark 14:33–42). G. Campbell Morgan points out that each of these three events has to do with death. In the home of Jairus, Jesus proved He was Master over death; on the mount of transfiguration He revealed that He would be glorified in His death; and in the Garden He was submissive to death. Certainly James learned and remembered these lessons, and his martyrdom was a triumphant experience that glorified the Lord.[1]

But something else is involved. One day James and John, through their mother, asked Jesus to give them the thrones on His right and left when He entered into His kingdom (Matt. 20:20–28; Mark 10:35–45). Jesus asked the broth-ers if they could drink the cup He was going to drink and go through the baptism He would experience on the cross, and they said that they could! Little did they realize that their request and their boast would bring suffering to their lives. James was the first apostle to be martyred, and John was the last apostle to die, after suffering in his exile on Patmos. Indeed, they did drink the cup and go through the baptism of suffering.

Are we the kind of devoted Christians who are dangerous to the work of the devil? Are we among his targets—or his helpers? Are we thinking God's thoughts or the world's thoughts? "Get behind me, Satan!" Jesus said to Peter. "You are a stumbling block to me; you do not have in mind the things of God, but the things of men" (Matt. 16:23). Imagine Satan thinking in and speaking through Christ's number one apostle!

Two Thrones

King Herod sat on his splendid royal throne in his royal robes, inaccessible to the people but demanding their obedience. Little did he realize that there was a higher and greater throne accessible to the humblest child of God. The believers who assembled in Mary's house were pleading at the throne of grace, asking the Lord to deliver His servant; and God heard and answered their prayers. *Never underestimate the power of a praying church!* There were many who met to pray (Acts 12:12), and they prayed earnestly all week (v. 5). This means that they agonized in prayer, even as Jesus did in the Garden (Luke 22:44). They were united in their praying, and they prayed specifically for Peter. The night before he was to be executed, they spent that whole night at the throne of grace. It seems that there was even some unbelief mixed with their prayers, for when there was a knocking at the door, they couldn't believe that it was really Peter (Acts 12:15)!

Whenever believers or congregations have needs, we usually try to work things out ourselves, and then we ask God to bless our feeble efforts. The last desperate thing we do is to pray, when prayer is the *first* thing we ought to do. "You do not have, because you do not ask God" (James 4:2). Whatever else our churches may be known for in America today, they're not known for their powerful prayer ministry. There are exceptions and we thank God for them. My friend Pastor Jim Cymbala of the Brooklyn Tabernacle, a church known for its effective prayer ministry, writes, "Yes, the roughness of inner-city life has pressed us to pray. . . . But is the rest of the country coasting along in fine shape? I think not."[2] Whether we're in the inner city, the suburbs, or in a rural town, God's people need to pray.

God's throne is a throne of grace, which means we can come at any time, with any need, and He will hear us. There's power in prayer, and when the saints get together to pray, that power increases. As a novice minister in my first pastorate, I sometimes felt helpless and bewildered; and my perplexity increased when the church voted to build a new sanctuary! It would take faith and sacrifice to complete the building, and I could see myself ending up in the hospital with a bad case of ulcers. But some of the dear saints encouraged me to meet with them weekly for prayer, and I can't tell you how many problems God solved for us as we were on our knees. They taught me the power of persistent and united prayer.

Herod thought he had a powerful throne, but God's throne is far greater than the throne of any earthly king. Herod had some armed soldiers who obeyed him, but the Lord has myriads of angels who do His bidding swiftly and successfully. God's angel even entered Peter's prison cell, unknown to the four special guards. Herod ruled over a small area, but the Lord is sovereign over everything. "The LORD has established his throne in heaven, and his kingdom rules over all" (Ps. 103:19). If that doesn't encourage us to pray, nothing will!

Well over a century ago, Charles Haddon Spurgeon told his London congregation, "Believing prayer, dictated of the Spirit, and presented through Jesus Christ, is truly the power of the church, and we cannot do without it."[3]

Two Promises

If you were scheduled to be executed the next morning, how well would you sleep the night before? Peter slept so soundly that night that the angel had to strike him on the side to wake him up (Acts 12:7)! (If you want the privilege of having an angel for an alarm clock, you must be willing to go to prison for Jesus' sake.) Peter wasn't sleeping on a soft mattress—he was chained to two guards, hardly the best arrangements for a restful night of sleep. A guard stood at each of the two prison doors, because Herod wasn't going to have Peter escape the way he and his friends did the last time. He assigned sixteen soldiers to guard Peter during the night, but all of Herod's calculations proved futile.

What was the secret of Peter's sound sleep? He knew that he would not be killed. What gave him that confidence? He believed the promise Jesus gave him when He restored him to fellowship and discipleship:

> "I tell you the truth, when you were younger you dressed yourself and went out where you wanted; but when you are old you will stretch out your hands, and someone will dress you and lead you where you do not want to go." Jesus said this to indicate the kind of death by which Peter would glorify God.
>
> John 21:18–19

Our Lord was describing death by crucifixion, and Herod's mode of execution was decapitation by the sword. Knowing that the Lord's word could never be broken, Peter rested his head on the pillow of that promise and fell sound asleep. Perhaps he remembered how Jesus went to sleep in the boat during the storm, and this encouraged him (Mark 4:38).

But there was another promise that must have been especially meaningful to Peter, because he quoted it in his first epistle: "For the eyes of the Lord are on the righteous and his ears are attentive to their prayer, but the face of the Lord is against those who do evil" (1 Peter 3:12). This promise comes from Psalm 34:15–16, and I suggest you stop and read that entire psalm and consider it in the light of Peter's situation. God's eyes were on Peter, and His ears were open to the prayers of Peter's friends at the house of Mary. God did turn His face against that monster Herod and judge him for his many sins.

It's worth noting that this is the third occasion recorded in Scripture when Peter was asleep. The first was on the mount of transfiguration, and he woke up to see the glory of God (Luke 9:32). He also went to sleep while Jesus was praying in the Garden (Luke 22:45), and he awakened just in time to pull out the sword and start to fight. In Herod's prison, Peter woke up to see an angel, who led him out to freedom. In the first two instances, Peter wasn't quite ready to face reality, and, consequently, said and did the wrong thing. But in the prison, he quietly obeyed the angel's instructions. Peter at least learned from his past mistakes.

You and I need to rest on what Peter called God's "very great and precious promises" (2 Peter 1:4). God waited until almost the last minute to deliver Peter, but Peter knew that "the Lord is not slow in keeping his promise" (2 Peter 3:9). God's children don't live on explanations; we live on promises. If Paul is the apostle of faith and John the apostle of love, Peter is the apostle of hope. Our faith and hope are in God (1 Peter 1:21), and it's a "living hope" because we trust a living Savior (v. 3). "Set your hope fully on the grace to be given you when Jesus Christ is revealed" (v. 13). The hope we have is a reasonable one, and we don't have to be ashamed of it (3:15).

Two Exoduses

Peter's arrest took place at Passover, when the Jews were celebrating their deliverance from Egypt. The focus of attention at Passover was the innocent lamb that would give its life for the redemption of the people. Peter knew that the real Lamb was Jesus: "Christ, our Passover lamb, has been sacrificed" for us (1 Cor. 5:7), and Peter called Him "a lamb without blemish or defect" (1 Peter 1:19). Our Lord's work of redemption on the cross is called "his departure, which he was about to bring to fulfillment at Jerusalem" (Luke 9:31), and, as we learned earlier, *departure* is the Greek word *exodos* (see also 2 Peter 1:15). God's people need not fear death; it's but a release from the bondage of this life and an entrance into the presence of God.

But Peter experienced his own exodus that night as the angel set him free and led him out of the prison. While the Jewish people in Jerusalem were looking back and remembering the birth of their nation on Passover night, Peter was looking ahead and following the angel to freedom. The chains fell from his wrists, so he was able to put on his clothes and his sandals, and then the doors opened automatically so Peter could get out. Once he was outside, Peter no longer needed miracles, so the angel departed; and Peter headed for the home of Mary, mother of Mark.

The Old Testament Jewish believer measured everything by the power God displayed at the exodus, but the New Testament Christian looks to the empty tomb and the ascended Christ seated on the throne in heaven (Eph. 1:15–23). Jesus has all power and all authority to use it, and nothing is too hard for Him to accomplish. Charles Wesley saw in Peter's prison experience a picture of his own conversion to Christ:

> Long my imprisoned spirit lay
> Fast bound in sin and nature's night;
> Thine eye diffused a quick'ning ray,
> I woke, the dungeon flamed with light;
> My chains fell off, my heart was free;
> I rose, went forth, and followed Thee.[4]

Our "salvation exodus" through the blood of the Lamb is just the beginning, because the resurrection power of Jesus Christ is available to us as we trust Him and yield to the Holy Spirit. What we read as Peter's story can be our story.

"Anyone can do the possible," wrote A. W. Tozer; "add a bit of courage and zeal and some may do the phenomenal; only Christians are obliged to do the impossible."[5] And that's where prayer and the power of God come in.

Two Surprises

Peter must have known that the saints were praying for him at Mary's house, because that's where he went. The angel didn't tell him what to do; it was Peter's decision, and it was a wise one. Mary's son John Mark had been led to Christ by Peter (1 Peter 5:13), and Peter was well acquainted with the household. The fact that the servant Rhoda recognized his voice indicates this. Perhaps Peter led both Mark and Rhoda to the Savior and taught them the Word whenever he visited Mary. It would be just like Peter to pay attention to a lowly servant. In Christ, there is no difference between male and female or bond and free (Gal. 3:26–28).

The first surprise is that Rhoda left Peter standing at the door (Acts 12:14)! A servant's job is to open the door to guests, but she was so overcome with joy that she kept him waiting while she delivered the good news. Joy can do that to us, especially the joy of answered prayer. But it wasn't wise to keep Peter standing outside. The sooner he was inside the house, the safer he would be. The emotions of the moment must never hinder us from doing the work God has assigned us to do.

However, we need to consider the part that Rhoda played in this event. She must have had a keen ear to detect Peter's voice through the door, but suppose it had been one of Herod's soldiers impersonating Peter? Wasn't Rhoda putting everybody in danger by affirming it was Peter when she hadn't even seen him? Perhaps, but both her ear and her heart told her who it was, and she was right.

The second surprise is that the saints didn't really expect to see Peter! They thought that either Rhoda had lost her mind or that Peter's guardian angel was at the door to announce his death. But angels don't have to knock—they just walk right in. The believers had been faithful to pray for Peter, and God heard their supplications even though He knew that some of the people doubted that He would answer. How gracious of God to answer our prayers even when they're mingled with unbelief! Not every answer to prayer indicates that the people praying are worthy. God gives what we request because the answer glorifies His name and accomplishes His purposes on earth.

That was an unforgettable Passover for Peter, Mary, Mark, Rhoda, and their praying friends. But every day is unforgettable if we pray, walk by faith, and keep listening and looking for God's surprising answers.

Epilogue

YES, LIFE CAN BE A MIRACLE!

*A*s I've pondered the life of Peter and considered the miracles he experienced, one statement from his first letter has repeatedly come to my mind: "Cast all your anxiety on him because he cares for you" (1 Peter 5:7).

Christians do have cares and anxieties, in spite of what some people think and some preachers preach. Peter had his disappointments in business, like fishing all night and catching nothing. Once he had a sick mother-in-law, and one night he almost drowned. He had to pay his temple tax and had no money. Late one night he attacked a man with his sword and cut off the man's ear. He denied Jesus three times and thought he had reached the end of the road. Innocent as he was, Peter even spent a week in prison.

But Peter knew Jesus, and Jesus cared enough for him to help solve his problems and meet his needs.

"He cares for you"—four monosyllables—is such a simple statement, yet at the same time it's so profound. Why should Jesus care for me and for you? "What is man that you are mindful of him, the son of man that you care for him?" (Ps. 8:4). All of creation shouts to us, "God cares! He cares!" Noah saw it in the rainbow and Jesus in the birds and the flowers. The Bible speaks to us faithfully and says, "God cares for you!" But if you ever doubt that God cares for you, go by faith to the cross and see Jesus dying for you. "He who did not spare his own Son, but gave him up for us all—how will he not also, along with him, graciously give us all things?" (Rom. 8:32). Calvary whispers to our hearts in the still small voice of love, "I care."

Our responsibility is to believe this remarkable truth and act on it by entrusting everything to Him. Once and for all, turn everything over to Him, and then trust Him and do what He says. He doesn't work in spite of us or instead of us; He works with us and in us and for us as we cooperate with Him. "If anyone serves, he should do it with the strength God provides, so that in all things God may be praised through Jesus Christ. To him be the glory and the power for ever and ever. Amen" (1 Peter 4:11).

Life is a school and Peter admonishes us to "grow in the grace and knowledge of our Lord and Savior Jesus Christ" (2 Peter 3:18). It's much easier to grow in knowledge than it is to grow in grace, and that's why the Lord sends us trials and permits us to get into difficult situations. These trying circumstances give us opportunities to translate learning into living as we trust Christ for what we need. We learn from our mistakes, but we also learn from our obedience. We get to know Jesus better, but we also get to know ourselves better, and both are important.

Dr. Bob Cook often told us in Youth for Christ, "Ask God to keep your life and ministry on a miracle basis."

That's the way Peter finally learned to live.

That's the way you and I can live.

NOTES

Prologue: *God's Second Greatest Miracle*

1. Stanley Hauerwas and William H. Willimon, *Resident Aliens* (Nashville: Abingdon Press, 1989), 65.

2. George H. Morrison, *Sunrise: Addresses from a City Pulpit* (London: Hodder and Stoughton, 1903), 88.

3. Watchman Nee, *A Table in the Wilderness* (Fort Washington, Pa: Christian Literature Crusade, 1965), 22 January.

Chapter 3: *Miracles Can Happen at Home*

1. Robert Frost, "The Death of the Hired Man," *Robert Frost's Poems*, with introduction and commentary by Louis Untermeyer (New York: Pocket Books, 1971), 165.

Chapter 5: *The Kingdom and the Glory*

1. William R. Moody, *The Life of Dwight L. Moody* (Grand Rapids: Revell, 1900), 552.

2. Ibid., 554–55.

Chapter 7: *God's Grace in the Garden*

1. A. W. Tozer, *We Travel An Appointed Way* (Tulsa, Okla.: Christian Publicating Services, 1988), 106.

Chapter 9: *Thanks for the Memory*

1. Some students emphasize the fact that Jesus used two different words for love: *phileo*, which means "friendship, love, and fondness," and *agapao*, which means "sacrificing love that is willed and not just emotional." But Peter and Jesus spoke in Aramaic, where these differences aren't found, and throughout

the Gospel of John, the writer used the two words interchangeably. Our Lord knew that neither Peter nor any other believer could have the same kind of love for God that God has for us.

2. Newton, John, *Voice of the Heart* (Chicago: Moody Press, 1950), 288.

3. Thomas Shepherd, "Must Jesus Bear the Cross Alone?" in *Worship and Service Hymnal* (Chicago: Hope Publishing Co., 1957), no. 349.

Chapter 11: *Me and My Shadow*

1. Jean-Marc Pottiez, ed., *Feather Fall* (Morrow, 1994), 17.

2. James M. Kouzes and Barry Z. Posner, *The Leadership Challenge* (Jossey-Bass, 1987), 16.

Chapter 13: *Waking Up to Miracles!*

1. G. Campbell Morgan, *The Crises of the Christ* (Grand Rapids: Revell, 1903), 249.

2. Jim Cymbala with Dean Merrill, *Fresh Wind, Fresh Fire* (Grand Rapids: Zondervan, 1997), 49. I recommend this book, and its sequel *Fresh Faith*, to any Christian or church that needs the prayer life strengthened.

3. *The Metropolitan Tabernacle Pulpit* (Pilgrim Publications, 1980), vol. 21, 437.

4. Charles Wesley, "And Can It Be That I Should Gain?" in *Worship and Service Hymnal*, no. 259.

5. A. W. Tozer, *The Warfare of the Spirit* (Camp Hill, Pa: Christian Publications, 1993), 12.

Warren W. Wiersbe is Distinguished Professor of Preaching at Grand Rapids Baptist Seminary and has pastored churches in Indiana, Kentucky, and Illinois (Chicago's historic Moody Memorial). He is the author and editor of more than one hundred books and now focuses his energies on writing, teaching, and conference ministry.